Talking with the Animals

Adele Beesley, an Indiana farm woman, with an injured grosbeak she nursed back to health and returned to the wild.

Talking with the Animals

How to Communicate with Wildlife

by **Bill Thomas**

Photographs by Bill Thomas

William Morrow and Company, Inc. / New York

Library of Congress Cataloging in Publication Data

Thomas, Bill, 1934–
    Talking with the animals.

    Includes index.
    1. Human-animal communication.   2. Wildlife watching.
3. Tracking and trailing.   I. Title.
QL776.T46   1985   591'.072   84–27163
ISBN 0-688-02844-6

Printed in the United States of America

First Edition

1 2 3 4 5 6 7 8 9 10

BOOK DESIGN BY ARLENE GOLDBERG

Dedicated to the trillions of life forms with which we share our world and worlds beyond, and to humans who have developed a special rapport with and respect for all life.

Contents

1. Communicating with Animals   9
2. Animal Talk   30
3. The Role of Man in His Environment   49
4. The Role of the Hunter   62
5. Learning to See   81
6. Learning to Walk and Stalk   104
7. Reading Signs   118
8. Learning to Listen; Developing a Sense of Smell 133
9. That Amazing Sixth Sense   151
10. Wisdom of the Weeds   168
11. Capturing Images   184
12. Training   203
13. "Ask now the beasts, and they shall
    teach thee"   225
    List of Prime Wildlife Areas   244
    Photo Workshops   248
    Index   249

Chapter 1

Communicating with Animals

$\mathcal{M}$orning draped an abandoned streambed of the Rio Grande with an unusually fine mist as I awakened, climbed from my small motorhome, and stumbled down the trail toward the muddy river. Rounding a bend toward the barely audible sounds of softly running water, I came suddenly face to face with one of the largest rattlesnakes I'd encountered in a decade. Coiled loosely, almost cuddled, it lay squarely across the trail, a temporary resting place chosen sometime during the night.

The day was yet cool—the sun had just burst across the horizon from behind a heavy cloud cover. This big fellow was obviously cool, comfortable, and not anxious to move aside. I wasn't about to crowd him. For five minutes, I squatted peering into the slit-pupil eyes, studying the gentle curvature of the thick-scaled body. It was a fine specimen, with colorful markings—a true western diamondback.

Never having met a western diamondback face to face in

How intelligent is a raccoon?

broad daylight before, it was an encounter I shall cherish the remainder of my life. During the next two hours, this critter and I would get to know each other better. At least I hoped we would, as I rushed back to my motorhome to round up all the camera gear I could get my hands on. Although he was still in deep shadow from tall willows nearby when I returned, the sun would soon shorten the shadows and I would be able to work with him.

During the best part of the morning, this five-foot-long rattler and I developed a kinship I shall never forget. I teased him, took chances I had no business taking, attempted to get him to strike the camera for that dramatic front-on shot of a rattler's bared fangs, uncoiled him with a short stick. Finally, when he could take all this harassment no longer, he tried to retreat to the clump of nearby willows.

A couple of aged tourists came down the trail: a gaunt, thin man in dress trousers and a sweater, and a plump lady in a two-piece Perma-press.

"Be careful!" I warned. "We have a rattler here."

The fat woman screamed and turned tail immediately, heading in the other direction at a fast pace. Her husband stood his ground, but I could see his upper lip quiver just a bit as he peered over my shoulder attempting to satisfy his curiosity. "Snakes," he said shakily, "scare my wife to death."

During my entire morning with this western diamondback, I believed there was more transpiring between us than was immediately obvious. Not once, regardless of what I did to him (and I never struck him, but handled him as gently as possible), did he threaten to bite me. He rattled sometimes, and on a couple of occasions offered a halfhearted strike with the mouth closed, as though to ask me to go away and leave him alone. I never did, so he finally determined to leave. In spite of my efforts to head him off, he slid past me into willow thickets so dense it would have been impossible to follow.

In the years since I was a small child on my father's Kentucky hill farm, I've met a lot of snakes, many of them venomous. Not during a single experience, however, have I been threatened or struck. I do have a healthy respect for all snakes—all of them—poisonous or nonpoisonous. Though I prefer not to handle them, I certainly have no dislike for them. In fact, I very much like snakes and other reptiles, but in their own element.

A few years ago when I was doing field research for my illustrated book, *The Swamp,* I spent months wading around in swamps throughout many parts of the United States. Snakes were daily companions. I walked, canoed, waded, swam in their domain. They were all around me much of the time. One day in the Florida Everglades I met a tiny pygmy rattler, no more than ten inches long. The snake refused to coil. Although I sought to make it do so for capturing on film, I was never successful. Finally, with an almost inaudible warning buzz from the minuscule rattlers, it retreated into a tall clump of grass and hid. I could have fished it out, but decided to leave it alone. I had already gotten pictures of it docilely lying beside the trail, a disgusting image for a snake that's supposed to be aggressive and dangerous.

Encounters with all kinds of animals have occurred across most of this continent during the past quarter century of my life—bear, Gila monster, moose, elk, otter, whales, and a multitude of birds. Reactions have been varied, both on my part and on the part of the creatures. In many cases, the creatures have stood their ground or continued their activity as though I were not present. The greater the number of such encounters, the more I must ask the question, Why?

Were they not fearful because they sensed I posed no threat? Did they realize I was armed only with cameras, not guns or bows and arrows? And was this feeling, if there were indeed such a feeling, conveyed by electromagnetic means, by pheromones, or by some other signal of which I was not consciously aware? Or was it simply because I talked to them?

Dr. Thomas Sebeok, director of the Research Center for Animal Communications at Indiana University, an internationally known authority on the subject, does not believe any sort of sixth sense exists either in man or in animals. Instead, he believes all such communications and resulting reactions are based on clues that come through hearing, scent, or sight.

12

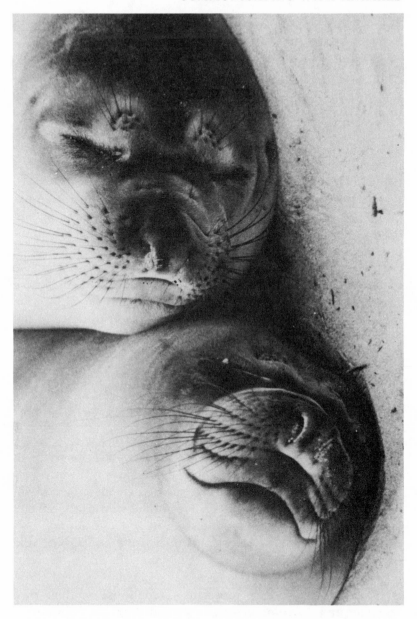

Marine mammals, like these baby elephant seals on a California beach, are believed to have a high degree of intelligence.

13

"Creatures read signals from us," he said, "signs that aren't even apparent to us. They pick up the slightest movement or odor, indications that give away our thought patterns. Animals—perhaps other living forms, too—are able to interpret and act upon those signals, sometimes with split-second timing."

While it was once believed that animals reacted purely by instinct, like programmed robots, today we know that unquestionably many factors enter into animal—or creature—behavior. By no means is communication limited to animals, insects, or even marine creatures. Some very impressive experiments have been carried out in the botanical kingdom through the use of magnetic electrodes, for instance, which indicate that plants also react to certain external stimuli. Among higher forms of life, researchers continue to find considerable evidence that in addition to heredity, environment has a strong bearing upon behavior. Moreover, even within the same species no two animals can be expected to react in the same manner to a particular encounter. They are individuals, as much as human beings are individuals, and may react in totally different ways.

Human interest in other living species upon the planet has never been greater. But understanding these other creatures was little further advanced at the turn of this century than it was during the time of ancient man. Only very recently has a new science been developed to deal with the study of animal behavior. We call it *ethology*. In some ways ethology resembles old-fashioned natural history, for both subjects concern creatures as they live their lives in the wild. But ethology is almost as new as the Atomic Age; its use of scientific procedures and devices produces a picture of the insect, bird, and animal world far more accurate than that shown in the writings of Victorian naturalists. Especially fascinating are the ethological studies on how conscious animals are of their own behavior and, therefore, capable of choosing among options.

Much current interest lies in the study of pheromones— the various scents induced by internal or, in some cases, external stimuli that affect behavior. Well-known examples of

14

pheromones are the sex attractants produced by the females of many species of bees, beetles, and moths to attract males. Evidence is mounting regarding the role pheromones and other odors play in the higher forms of life, including humans. Some people go so far as to claim that vegetarians are able to establish greater rapport with animals simply because they smell differently. According to this theory, the body odor transmitted by vegetarians is noticeably more tolerable to most animals than that of meat-eaters. This stands to reason, too, the theory claims, since it's an established fact that animals possess greater defensive attitudes toward another creature that may indeed devour them.

This theory, while untested, would seem to make sense. I find it much easier to work with vegetarian animals with confidence—even though they may be several times my size—simply because I know they have no interest in choosing me for lunch. For instance, a working session with manatees, sometimes known as sea cows, at a Florida location was not at all worrisome to me—even though the manatees weighed up to nearly a ton each—because they are vegetarian. To watch half a dozen of these huge creatures looming up ahead of you in the water, moving steadily toward you, and sometimes actually rubbing against you, could be a harrowing experience were they meat-eaters. If you don't believe there's a difference, try it sometime with a blue-tip or great white shark of the same size.

Another aspect of behavior you must deal with if you want to get to know wildlife is migration and/or hibernation. Bears and many other animals den up and restrict their activities in very cold weather. As the seasons change, many creatures—both large and small—migrate long distances to extreme geographical locations. Certain birds may stay in your area all year, but most you will see only seasonally or during their migrations, and still others may not migrate through your area at all. Some insect species such as the monarch butterfly make the trip but once; their offspring replace them the following year. Pacific salmon are born in freshwater streams, find their way ultimately to the ocean, make one grand sweep

15

It's worth overcoming a fear of snakes to enjoy beautiful creatures like this cottonmouth moccasin I caught in my lens in the Florida panhandle.

of the Pacific, and several years later, return precisely not only to the same stream where they were born but to the same tributary pool. There they may deposit their eggs and die.

In many cases, these journeys of migration are almost unbelievable, and relatively little is known about them. A number of puzzling factors confront the scientists. How does the tiny hummingbird, for instance, burning unbelievable energy, make the journey across the Gulf of Mexico into South America? And indeed, how does the monarch butterfly—at least those migrating down the east coast—make the trip across the Gulf of Mexico, more than five hundred miles over ocean and through a hostile environment, to its winter home in Mexico?

Just how intelligent are the various forms of wildlife? Are

16

they able to develop new directions of creativity? Do they use tools? Do they speak a language between themselves which may serve just as well as, if not better than, that of humanity?

Some psychologists believe certain animals possess a high degree of intelligence. Take deer, for instance. They do not burrow, nor do they build shelters. They weather the worst of the elements, including temperatures well below zero or a terrain frozen in snow and ice, and protect themselves against the constant threat of predators, including man, wild and domestic dogs. Every creature of the wilds is day to day, moment to moment, pitted against the challenges of its world. That animals continue to survive even under adverse conditions may indicate a greater degree of awareness and adaptability than they were once given credit for.

For many of us, the gap in our interpretation of wildlife behavior is bridged by our interest in intelligence. One winter day when I was carrying up wood from my backyard for the fireplace, my dog—a four-year-old German shepherd with no special training—grabbed a piece of wood in his mouth and carried it up on the deck, placing it beside the stack I had started. Three trips I made and three trips he made, each time bringing up as large a piece of wood as he could muster, without any coaching from me.

A few years back near the Oklawaha River east of Ocala, Florida, I was trying a new French-made moped I had just purchased. A loop road led off the parking lot for the boat ramp and circled through the trees past the manager's residence and back out on the main road again. Twice I sped past the manager's house and each time a long-haired mongrel dog rushed out to attack me. The third time I came by, the manager stopped me.

"Don't ride this direction past here," he said. "This is a one-way drive heading the other way. The dog knows it's a one-way drive leading the other way and anyone heading the wrong way on it gets him highly upset. Turn around and ride the other way around the loop and he won't bother you."

I did, and the dog never came after me again.

The proliferation of ethologists and wildlife observers is

17

Pheromones may play a role in how close we can get to animals such as this hoary marmot in Alaska.

now providing increasing examples of similar intelligence in the natural kingdom.

Jane Goodall, in her work with chimpanzees in East Africa, reported numerous instances in which they used sticks and branches as tools to procure food they could not otherwise reach. The sea otter dives for crustaceans but is unable to open the shells. So it gathers a suitable rock from the bottom of the ocean, swims to the surface, lies on its back in the water, and pounds the shell open with the rock. Egyptian vultures have been observed tossing rocks at ostrich eggs they couldn't otherwise break open to eat.

Observers of wolves and coyotes have noted the use of "drive animals," utilized by the pack to drive the quarry into an ambush at an opportune time and place. Studies of wild dogs, hyenas, and other predators in Africa have shown such complex hunting patterns that observers question whether conscious cooperation is not involved. Even pigeons have been found capable of discriminating between geometric patterns and drawings of actual objects such as a tree or a person. The science of underwater photography is revealing amazing behavior among fish, for example, one species that uses other species as a shield when sneaking up on its prey.

Much evidence of individualism within species is also emerging. Hawks, for instance, usually kill their prey with their talons or beaks, sometimes depending upon their awesome mid-air impact to stun the quarry or to break its neck. Yet in several documented cases, hawks have taken the easy way out by settling in shallow water and calmly holding the prey under water to drown. Even examples of art exist among fish and birds, the most spectacular being the bowerbird of New Guinea, which uses flowers and other decorative materials to construct a huge bower for its mate. Though male birds construct bowers and most seem to favor the color blue, there is no set pattern—the bowers vary in width from only a couple of feet to eight feet and no two are alike in either colors or materials used.

Such experiences and examples have led me to believe without doubt that many creatures do possess a good deal of

19

intelligence. Though their languages, their principles, their basic way of life are all different from ours, that does not give me the right to discount their ability to think or to act on thought.

And what about this thing we call instinct? Do animals really possess instinct? And do we human beings also possess it? Did our ancestors, or ancient man, possess instinctive powers? And last, if we do have instincts, do we share with animals a common response to kindness? Do all creatures everywhere respond to kindness, kind thoughts as well as kind actions? When I think of wild creatures responding to kindness, I recall a slight, unassuming little lady named Grace Wiley who did some wonderful things with reptiles at her Zoo for Happiness near Long Beach, California. She was considered one of the world's leading herpetologists, and she certainly had a way with snakes.

Among her wards at the zoo were enormous king cobras, adders, copperheads, Australian black snakes, green mambas, fer-de-lances, moccasins, and numerous types of rattlesnakes. People were fascinated by Miss Wiley and her zoo; they came for miles to watch her work. Her daily talks, as she stood coddling a poisonous snake in her arms, were most popular. Interpreting the snakes from their own point of view, she would show fascinated audiences what splendid philosophical teachers and companions snakes can be when given the opportunity. She would usually close her talks with the observation that deep within his heart the snake is not a troublemaker at all but a fine gentleman; when he strikes, he does so because someone with evil intent has invaded his domain and cornered, frightened, or hurt him.

People loved to watch Miss Wiley work with snakes. A feature of the zoo was the "gentling room," in which newcomers were brought for an introduction to Miss Wiley. Through a glass window, crowds could watch Miss Wiley enter this nearly bare room and take her position seated at the far end of a table. She would become motionless. In each hand she held an odd-looking stick about three feet long. One of

20

Birds, like this rooster pheasant in Nebraska, often respond to signals we may not be aware of.

these had a cuplike mesh arrangement at the end; the other, padded with soft cloth, was known as the petting stick.

On the day that I happened to be watching, a large box with warning signs all over it was wheeled into the room and placed on the table. Loud, clattering, spine-tingling sounds coming through top and sides indicated the contents were a rattlesnake. When Miss Wiley nodded, the attendant jerked off the top and elevated one end of the box. Out into this new world slid Mr. Snake. He was over six feet in length, beautifully designed, filled with tremendous energy and ready for action.

The rattler immediately coiled into a steel spring, ready to strike at anything that moved. His tail rattled furious warnings. But nothing happened.

From the moment Miss Wiley saw the snake, she had been silently talking across to it. Outwardly she appeared to be doing nothing at all. Actually, she was proving the potency and effectiveness of her favorite rule of action in all relationship contacts: That all life, regardless of its form, classification, or reputation, will respond to genuine interest, respect, admiration, appreciation, affection, gentleness, courtesy, good manners. That's what she preached. And this big rattler, excited and angered, was being lovingly showered with these qualities, perhaps for the first time in its entire life.

Had I been able to listen to this silent talk, I would have heard her praising the snake for its many excellent qualities, assuring it that it had absolutely nothing to fear, and reminding it again and again that it simply had come to a new home where it would always be appreciated, loved, and cared for. All of this was communicated without the slightest sound or movement.

Within minutes, observers began to notice a marked change in the snake's attitude. The frantic rattling of its tail slowed. Its head, which had been glaring in all directions at a fast, nervous tempo, steadied itself in the direction of Miss Wiley, even though it could not clearly distinguish her shape from the wall behind her. This "killer" from Texas was not

22

only receiving but actually responding to the friendly thoughts and feelings being sent in its direction.

Now Miss Wiley began to talk to it in soft, low tones. Slowly the big snake began to uncoil and cautiously stretch itself the full length of the table, finally resting its head within inches of where Miss Wiley was seated. Then came the first physical movement. Miss Wiley reached across and began gently stroking the snake's back, in the beginning with the soft-padded petting stick and then, since there was no resistance, with her two bare hands. And as you watched this unbelievable performance, you could see this Texas wild snake actually arch its long back in catlike undulations. All accomplished within a few minutes, utilizing what Miss Wiley called a simple formula for understanding wild creatures.

While Grace Wiley was an impressive expert in handling snakes, it must be remembered there are exceptions to every rule. Ironically, neither the zoo nor Miss Wiley is any longer there. Miss Wiley was bitten by a cobra and died, and the zoo went out of business.

Without animals, mankind would be lost. Aside from their obvious practical uses such as serving as a source of food, they fill a valuable niche in the world of all of us. Think of a world without birds, butterflies, squirrels or deer. How dull it would indeed be. Wildlife provides, among other things, a vital link between ourselves and reality. Wildlife watching involves more than just observing: it establishes a relationship that helps to fulfill our own lives.

Although it concerns domestic animals, the following study points up the role the animal world can play in the lives of humans. A few years ago at a Baltimore hospital, twenty-eight women and sixty-four men became participants in a research project involving pets. All had been hospitalized because of serious heart disease. Dr. Erika Friedmann intensively investigated many factors affecting their lifestyles—social contacts, environmental stress, economic status, and other matters that might play a role in their illness. Of the ninety-two patients, thirty-nine did not own pets. Within a year, eleven of those thirty-nine had died; but only three of those who had pets passed away. Dr. Friedmann has since recommended pet ownership as a therapeutic tool.

In another case at the Ohio State University Department of Psychology, a project establishing dogs in the psychiatric wards of mental hospitals and in nursing homes was tried. Almost immediately, some of the patients—even those who had been totally uncommunicative up to that point—began asking to play with or help take care of the dogs.

The study, under the direction of Dr. Samual Corson, selected fifty of the most seriously ill patients who had not responded to any other form of psychiatric treatment. Only three refused to accept a dog. All the others soon were showing remarkable degrees of improvement, and several thereafter recovered enough to be released.

"There is no question," says Dr. Corson, "the dogs made all the difference in the world. You could just measure attitude changes, and the overall outlook became so much more positive."

Although there is a lack of documentary studies, interest in wildlife by both the mentally retarded and the physically handicapped person has created marked changes in attitude. In wildlife sanctuaries across the land which provide facilities for the handicapped, I've witnessed persons in wheelchairs thoroughly enjoying themselves bird-watching or studying animal habitat or behavior. Bird watching is especially beneficial, for what could brighten the day of a wheelchair victim more than sitting beside a beaver pond watching the activity? At the Great Swamp National Wildlife Refuge just beyond the busy traffic hum of Greater New York City, I once observed several wheelchair victims, binoculars and identification books in hand, studying the antics of a family of wild Canada geese from the elevated boardwalk one spring. Not only does such observation provide relaxation and a sense of accomplishment for the handicapped; it works for the rest of us, too.

The quest for greater knowledge about animal behavior, of course, is not new. In fact, it is as old as the fossilized remains of very early man. The fossils tell that our ancestors in

The scolding of crows is often a clue that a hawk or owl is nearby. I photographed this barred owl in Indiana.

Africa lived at least partly on meat, cracking open bones to get at the marrow of scavanged animals or those they killed. Human beings have always been able to live entirely on vegetable foods, and millions do so now. In most civilizations, however, when mammals, fish, birds, or even insects have been available, man has generally been in part carnivorous. So man has always been keenly interested in other animals for one very basic reason: He wants to eat them.

But the fact that man from very early on was fascinated with other creatures aside from their food value is evident from the ancient drawings found on the walls of caves or on protected rock surfaces. Some artists modeled animal likenesses from clay or carved figurines of bone or stone; evidence also exists of metal and clay fashioned into animal and human figures before these materials were used to make weapons or pots. Among the hundreds of prehistoric drawings in the Lascaux Cave at Montignac, in France, one particularly interesting rendition shows a bison and a man. The bison is realistic; the man figure is not, for the head is that of a bird. Near the man's right hand is a stick bearing the figure of a bird. Thus some 15,000 years ago, a Stone Age artist documented his own belief—and perhaps that of his peers—in a mystical kinship between man and beast.

The belief continued. In the pre-Columbian era in the New World, native Americans revered many creatures. These became his brothers of the wild and turned up in many forms of art. The bison, the great thunderbird (in some areas the eagle and in others the California condor), the deer, the wolf, the bear, the otter, the jaguar, the snake—all these creatures lived in close proximity to the early people of our hemisphere. The social unity of the tribe was often based on the ghostly presence of an animal ancestor. Its likeness might be tattooed on tribal members or appeared on masks, weapons, pottery, and buildings. In some places in North and South America gigantic animal figures—so large they are only fully appreciated from aerial views, as a god might see them—were painstakingly fashioned of stones, earth mounds, or other materials. Taboos sometimes prevented the killing or eating of the totemic animal. This is still true today for some of the tribes of the Pacific Northwest, Alaska, and South America.

Because early man hunted animals, he came to know and understand them, and in many cases, to more highly respect them. Even today, many avid hunters do not kill out of passion or hatred, but seek out their prey with respect, and often admiration. The Bible makes frequent mention of man's relationship with "the fish of the sea . . . the fowl of the air, and . . . every creeping thing that creepeth upon the earth." Even biblical laws decreeing kindness to animals are a cultural source of some of our humane legislation.

Our tradition of respect for animals can also be traced to the ancient Near East. Statues of animals were proudly displayed in Mesopotamia and some rulers kept wild animals as pets. Probably no ancient people loved animals more than did the Egyptians. Among many animals they considered sacred were the ibis and the crocodile, which were kept on public display. When they died, these as well as household pets like cats, were embalmed as carefully as were the human dead, and their mummies preserved in vast mausoleums.

Two researchers—Niko Tinbergen and Konrad Lorenz, both winners of the Nobel Prize for Medicine in 1973—are generally credited with founding the new science of ethology. Dr. Tinbergen's career dates back to a summer day when he wondered, after watching hundreds of wasps return to their colony, how each found its own particular burrow. And Dr. Lorenz has, upon numerous occasions, voiced his belief that "our fellow creatures can tell us the most beautiful stories."

The science of ethology is based in part upon the philosophy that all life shares a kindred spirit, that indeed there is an intimate relationship between all forms of being. One cannot come to understand a tiny grain of sand upon an isolated beach without some consideration of the farthest star in the heavens on a summer night.

Dr. B. F. Skinner, who is perhaps the leading American specialist in animal behavior, has gone another step further, showing how a knowledge of animal behavior can lead to

Like many animals, this bullfrog will probably be aware of you long before you see him.

greater understanding of human behavior. To know our friends—the thousands upon thousands of creatures that cohabit the planet with us—is to better know ourselves.

But to achieve such self-knowledge, we must spend much time and effort developing a relationship with other living things. Fortunately, it need not be concentrated, for every experience can be a positive learning adventure. While we may find all kinds of creatures—and plants as well—around us for much of the time, there are certain areas where greater concentrations occur, allowing easier access for learning about creatures of the wild kingdom. Among these are the national wildlife refuges, national parks, state game sanctuaries, serpentariums, aquariums, national forests, wilderness areas, state, regional, county, and city parks, as well as private wildlife sanctuaries. A list of Prime Wildlife Areas is published at the end of this book. Learn where they are, what each has to offer, and the types of wildlife most likely to be found there. Then introduce yourself to these areas and to the many creatures that inhabit them.

Chapter 2

Animal Talk

"Absolutely absurd," a visiting friend from an eastern city remarked when I told him one day I'd been out listening to the animals talk. He thought I was joking until I continued by telling him what they were saying. I could see disbelief mixed with inquisitiveness written all over his face. "You can't be serious," he finally said.

Fact is, I was very serious. Not only do animals talk, but they fill the world about us with conversation. Every day our ears are bombarded with the sounds of nature—birds, insects, domestic pets and, in the proper circumstances, wild animals.

Even in the most highly urbanized environments house sparrows and finches nest and sing, and you'll find squirrels and frogs in parks. In New York City, for example, you can watch bats and chimney swifts hunting in Times Square and find an occasional raccoon on the outskirts. Peregrine falcons rear their young on several New York City bridges, and especially observant bird watchers have made such rare finds as an ovenbird taking a rest during migrating season in the shrubbery planted in front of an apartment building in Greenwich Village.

In the morning when I go walking or running through my woodland, I hear the talk of up to a dozen grouse, each clucking away in its own distinct language. Sometimes I hear coyotes yipping their last farewell to the night before curling up in their den to sleep for the day. A pileated woodpecker calls from the distance, and the woods, particularly during the warm weather months, are filled with the songs of birds.

Often there are crows (which, incidentally, have one of the most diverse vocabularies of all the bird kingdom) and red-tailed hawks calling from their spiraling flight overhead. From deeper in the woods, owls hoot. And there's the chatter of chipmunks. Sometimes, I've heard the squeals of young rabbits talking to their mothers; occasionally I come upon a small herd of whitetail deer.

Normally we think of deer as being quiet, but they are not. They, too, talk to one another. When there's alarm or curiosity mixed with possible danger, I've watched them snort to one another, striking one front hoof sharply against the ground. I call it the stomping language.

I learned a few years ago that songbirds, and practically everything else in the wild kingdom for that matter, divide up the planet like so much real estate being parceled into subdivisions. Many of them defend their piece of territory with conversation. The British ornithologist Eliot Howard, who studied the territorial instincts of birds for many years, says birds very definitely stake out their claims on real estate and are willing, in many instances, to fight to the end to hold it. He states further that he believes virtually all wild creatures do the same thing: stake out their own little territory against intrusion by any other of their species and perhaps several other species as well.

Males of many migrating bird species fly north each spring in advance of the females and each stakes out a piece of territory which shall belong to him. He stakes it out with song, defending its boundaries with belligerent ardor. Then the females arrive. If his holdings are secure, he has little difficulty getting a discriminating bride to join him.

While birds post their property by singing, most ground

*At Tom Brown's Wilderness Survival & Tracking School
students barter without vocalizing.*

animals, since they live in a world strongly associated with smell, do it by "demarcating," which means depositing a characteristic scent at the boundaries of their domain. Members of the cat family do it by urinating on certain objects—trees, rocks, an old log. Certain animals have a special gland designed for this sole purpose. Among some deer and antelope, a gland above the eye produces a strong-smelling oily substance which, rubbed off on twigs and branches, impregnates the whole dwelling place with a mark of ownership.

Communication between creatures of the wild kingdom is not confined to sound or hearing alone, nor does it just take place between creatures of like species. It most often involves several senses. But the predominant ones, according to most studies, are sound, sight, and touch.

One of the strangest communications between two different species occurs between a little African bird called a honey guide and the ratel, or honey badger. The bird loves the grubs of bees and wasps; the badger loves honey. But the honey guide cannot deal with thousands of infuriated bees; and the badger has such short legs it cannot make the long investigations needed to locate the hives. So these two most unlikely creatures team up. The honey guide flies around the forest until it finds a bee tree, then whizzes to the placidly waiting badger and dances over its head, speaking in shrill cries. The badger follows the bird and, safe in its sting-proof hide, rips the hive to pieces. Both bird and beast then settle down to feast.

Another unusual conversation occurs among arboreal ants in the tropics. They talk from tree to tree by tapping on the bark and leaves so vigorously it sounds like a rain shower—a kind of Morse code of the jungle.

During the early 1980s, Florida Institute of Technology biologist John Morris and a student, Cathy Steel, decided that if they could teach manatees to communicate warning signals to one another, they might help to prolong that endangered species. The major threat to the manatee are power boats that run over them before they're able to get out of the way.

When the two began their studies on how they might communicate with the manatee, however, they found that manatees already had a rich vocabulary of more than a thousand sounds, including a series of interplay and distress calls. Using underwater hydrophones and computers to identify the various sounds, they sorted their findings into thirteen categories, depending upon age and sex. All the tones intensified with immediate danger. Said Steel: "Their sounds relate to their moods or convey information. How specifically, we don't really know."

Then there's the case of Hoover, the talking seal of the New England Aquarium in Boston, who just started picking up

What is this whitetail fawn whispering?

human words and repeating them . . . and some of them, since the aquarium is located in a not-so-good neighborhood, weren't too repeatable, either. But he's very much to the point, and when he's tired of performing for visitors, he merely tells them forthrightly: "Get out of here." And they go.

Aquarium officials say they've never done anything to train the seal, but his unmistakable Boston accent and the fact that some of his words aren't so clean make them believe he was taught to speak by some nocturnal vagrant visiting his tank. There's no evidence that Hoover understands a single word he speaks.

In the Yukon Territory, I've listened to a whole variety of sounds made by wolves, ranging from howls, quavers, whines, grunts, and growls to yips, barks, and wails. Each of these sounds contained a number of variations, and I'm sure there were sounds there that were far above or below my level of hearing but that other canines, in general, could easily hear.

One winter night while sleeping in my basement office, I was awakened by my German shepherd whining and licking me in the face at 4 A.M. The house is well insulated and further insulation was provided by a good snow pack. But my dog wanted outside, and he communicated that to me, once he was sure I was awake, by running to the door and looking up at the handle. I arose and let him out. Once outside, he dashed into the woods growling and within a few minutes came back with another dog—a stray—that apparently had been prowling around in the dark. Somehow, the stray dog had communicated its presence to my dog, insulated as he was inside the house basement.

Remarkable? In a sense it is remarkable, but it's also, when you've worked with animals for a while, understandable. Some of my Yupik friends in the lower Yukon River delta of Alaska claim they can understand the wolves as easily as I can understand my dog, and they listen intently to what the wolves have to say. Farther into the Arctic, other Eskimos claim to rely upon the wolves to tell them when the caribou herds are moving, where they are, and in what direction they are headed. They claim the wolves set up a whole communica-

This manatee, or sea cow, from Florida, one of the gentlest creatures on earth, is endangered.

tion grapevine, passing the message from one pack to another for miles and miles in advance of the caribou migration. The language that tells of the migration is distinctly different from any other sound they make.

But wolves also communicate with each other by sight. A direct stare, with most canine creatures, is a threat. The dominant member of a wolf pack, for instance, can control his wards from a considerable distance with eye contact. If the leader stares intently at a subordinate, the latter generally will assume a submissive posture—lie or crouch down, sometimes belly up. Other times it merely drops its head and tail and turns either sidewise or away from the leader, like a human child that has been scolded.

36

The same thing may hold true with your dog. Try staring at it coldly sometime, in complete silence, when the dog's attention is attuned to you. It may not work well, or at all, since the dog is not used to being stared at by his master. But again it may, depending largely upon whether you have complete silence and are screened from outside interference. I've done it as an experiment with more than one dog and many times got the same results I've seen in wolf packs.

Touch is not as widely used in the animal world as the senses of sight and sound, and it varies in usage from species to species. Chimpanzees touch a great deal, sometimes in great affection. A huge amount of their leisure time is spent touching and caressing each other. Deer also touch a good deal, sometimes rubbing noses, licking one another, or, in the case of bucks, sparring. I've come upon bull moose in Alaska, several within the same herd, and watched as two young bulls, without any apparent anger whatsoever, decided to test the strength of the other by butting heads. But only after talking it over with grunts, low bellows, and a variety of other sounds and gestures. While the cows and other bulls stood by watching, the two young bulls would then back off and rush each other, time and again, sometimes locking antlers and making much noise, but neither seemingly intent upon hurting the other. And always, when I've witnessed this behavior, a third bull moose—usually one I presume to be the patriarch of the herd—stands by, head erect, as though refereeing the entire event.

The Atlantic bottlenose dolphin uses touch to a very great extent. If an infant loses contact with its mother, for instance, the mother emits several loud whistles and the infant usually returns to her side. But if the offspring is feeling too rambunctious and ignores the mother's calls, she may lightly push it under the water and hold it there until, wriggling and squirming, it is allowed to surface again.

Once I witnessed five dolphins off the Sanibel Island Causeway in the Florida Gulf playing pitch with a fairly large fish. The fish, which must have weighed seven or eight pounds, was dead, but the dolphins had formed a circle about twenty feet in diameter and were all facing each other passing the corpse from one to another. The one in possession would sometimes feign a pitch to another member of the circle, then quickly toss it to another unsuspecting one. For a good thirty minutes or so, I watched this behavior while listening to the many squeaks and shrieks emitted by the playful creatures.

After they tired of the game, I watched as they swam away, all of them touching side by side as they cruised through the water. Adult females often swim so closely together they touch; it is a means of defense. And dolphins, like primates, the researchers say, spend much of their leisure time stroking and nuzzling each other. It apparently helps to hold the group together.

Touching sometimes bridges the gap between animals and humans, too. Jane Goodall, during more than twenty years of field research with the chimpanzees of Tanzania, describes in her book *In the Shadow of Man* that her most rewarding experiences have been the instances of touching. She relates her early experiences of touching with David Greybeard, one of the most respected chimps, who would allow her to accompany him on many of his sojourns through the jungle, and when she was delayed, would wait for her to catch up to him, sometimes taking her by the hand.

Communication exists in all species—even in plants, as we discuss in another part of this book, and in insects. One of the most fascinating forms of communication I've witnessed in the insect world is that of the honeybees. When I was a child, I used to sit by the hour close to the beehives observing the comings and goings of these busy little creatures. Occasionally one would stop to look me over, buzzing around my face inquisitively. If I sat very still, it would usually go away. When one lingered and tried to land on my nose, I would shake my head as though to tell it, "No, this is not the place to land." And invariably it would go away.

But often, as I watched, a worker bee would alight on the deck or porch of the hive and do what I called a honey dance. First discovered in 1945 by the German biologist Karl von Frisch, the honey dance, sometimes referred to simply as the

Hoover, the talking seal at the New England Aquarium.

waggle dance, usually indicates a new source of nectar. After discovery, the worker bee comes home to do a figure dance, always the middle run of the figure-8, allowing the tail of the bee to point in the direction of the discovery. Dr. von Frisch believed that the position of the sun in relation to the straight run provided the orientation. While doing the dance, the bee shakes its body back and forth from thirteen to fifteen times per second, all the while making an audible buzzing sound with its wings. Furthermore, researchers have found that the straight-run portion of the dance is in direct correlation to the amount of time it would take to fly from the hive to the new discovery, meaning, of course, that bees can and do have some indication of time. And if bees do, it's likely that other creatures do as well.

Some scientists compare the waggle dance of the honeybee to the advanced stages of human language. And while the dance could be said to resemble a game of charades, it is much more to the point, much better organized, and far less diabolical. The target is spoken of in abstract terms, describing an object removed both in time and space. The method of communication, though limited, conveys the idea and fully resolves the problem.

Silent communication is a most interesting phenomenon. Anyone who had played charades can verify that. We've become so accustomed to communicating with one another vocally, it's a virtually overwhelming challenge to attempt doing without speech. Tom Brown, Jr., in his New Jersey survival and tracking school, asks his students to bring things from home with which to barter. Brown seats his students, who may number anywhere from thirty to fifty, around in a huge circle on the grass, all facing inward. Each student then builds before him a display of the things he or she has brought to barter. The catch is, all bartering must be done silently. No sounds whatsoever. It's one of the most interesting and challenging exercises of the course, for to trade an unwanted item for something one wants takes much communicating. Surprisingly, many exchanges do occur, however. And more is

Lobo wolves in Washington State communicate their social and pecking order through facial and body expression.

41

The cougar lays its ears back when it feels threatened or aggravated.

learned about communicating during that one session than one learns throughout the rest of the week.

Although the science of ethology and communication is still in its infancy, considerable strides are being made toward greater understanding of many species. At Indiana University, Dr. Michael Petersen of the School of Psychology has been working with Old World and Japanese macaques for more than ten years in an attempt to learn more about their communication. Through a series of tests, Dr. Petersen has discovered that monkeys, like humans, are influenced by an alpha and a beta side of the brain. He also has broken down certain sound codes among these primates and hopes someday to break the entire vocal and visual language utilized by these particular monkeys.

42

"They have a most interesting means of communicating," says Dr. Petersen, "which is as much visual as it is vocal. And they are intelligent, perhaps much more so than we have given them credit for being."

Petersen described a nonlaboratory event which he finds rather incredible. "One of our macaque monkeys took his lead chain [attached to a collar around the monkey's neck], did a half-hitch with one of the links, stuck it between the overhead members of his cage, and made himself a swing. If I had not witnessed that myself, I would not have believed it. And no one taught him to do that, either."

Dr. Petersen has already verified different dialects in his charges and he believes dialects may occur in many other creatures.

Dialects have been found in various birds and even in the song of the whale. Dr. William Cummings, former bio-acoustician at the Naval Ocean Systems Center in San Diego and now chief scientist at the San Diego Natural History Museum, has taken recordings of humpback whales on both the Pacific and the Atlantic coasts. When slowed down and run through a sound analyzer, Cummings found that the songs showed definite differences in dialect.

Even frogs have been found to possess dialects. A New Jersey cricket frog makes a slightly different sound from one from South Dakota. Furthermore, a female cricket frog born and raised in New Jersey, if serenaded simultaneously with tape recordings of both South Dakota and New Jersey dialects, will head for the loudspeaker with the New Jersey accent.

One of the most remarkable experiences of communication I've had came while working out a magazine assignment on an intriguing farm in North Carolina' sandhill country in the early 1960s. The story began in 1934 with Lockhart Gaddy, farmer and goose hunter. Every year the tradition in the Gaddy household was to have Thanksgiving and Christmas goose on the dinner table. And every year, Gaddy was a successful goose hunter . . . up until 1934, when he began to admire the beautiful Canada geese that came south during the winter so much, he decided he could shoot no more.

Lockhart Gaddy had some domesticated geese on his farm, and after he quit hunting, the Canada geese started to drop in for a visit on the pond. Then they began to stay. First winter there were nine. Gaddy said they went back and told all their friends until there were more and more each year. He began feeding them, and pretty soon, there were more than he could grow feed for on the farm. The pond was getting too small, too. So he bought corn from his neighbors and enlarged the pond. Tourists heard about this remarkable Gaddy's Goose Refuge and started coming to see the geese. Here they could walk among them, reach out and touch them, even though they were wild. The geese would actually eat from anyone's hand; yet on neighboring farms, they wouldn't let anyone within a quarter-mile range. At Gaddy's place, they felt safe.

The Gaddys, in order to defray the rising cost of feeding the geese, began charging an entry fee. Both geese and visitors continued to increase until there were nearly 30,000 Canada geese and about that many human visitors to see them each winter.

Then, in 1953, disaster struck. Lockhart Gaddy dropped dead of an apparent heart attack while feeding the geese near the pond. His wife, Hazel, said there was utter silence among the 10,000 geese there at that time.

Gaddy had asked to be buried on a mound not more than fifty feet from the pond in a grove of pine trees. His wishes were now carried out. On the day of the funeral, Mrs. Gaddy told me, the geese were again completely silent all through the funeral procession. After it was over and the people left, the geese came out of the pond and paraded to the grave, walking all around and over it time and again.

Mrs. Gaddy continued to run the refuge for many years afterward, until her death in the early 1970s, and the number of geese coming each year continued to increase until that time. Then a relative of the Gaddy's took over and attempted to run the refuge—but something had changed. The rapport was no longer there. The geese apparently communicated to one another that the Gaddys were no more and the number of geese arriving each year began to dwindle almost spon-

This Louisiana heron looks like it's dancing, but it's casting a shadow with its wings to attract fish.

taneously until 1975, when the refuge was closed permanently because no geese showed up. An era had come and gone. To this day, large V-formations of Canada geese continue to fly over during autumn en route to someplace else. Hardly ever does one of them stop.

More recently, much work has been under way with another form of intercourse: chemical communication, specifically, pheromones. Pheromones are prevalent among the insect world, but now researchers believe they play an important role in communication between all creatures, including wildlife reading the intentions of man.

In many animals, pheromones or chemical reactions have a major, often decisive role in communication or behavior. They are thought to play a major role in both honeybees and ants, which have some of the most complex social orders in the insect world. Researchers believe it's through pheromones that the ant and bee societies are able to remain organized in such close quarters; sensitivities and thoughts may be communicated and perceived automatically, without any effort being expended.

Chemical messages, research has shown, may be relayed from one individual to other individuals in the future, as in the homing instincts of salmon, which orient themselves by chemical underwater guideposts, creating one of the most remarkable sojourns known in the wild kingdom.

The chemical emissions of humans are something we may have overlooked, but to the super-sensitive wildlife accustomed to picking up phermones, man may indeed stink. The American Indians went so far as to say so when the first European settlers arrived. Later, when the Indians started wearing white men's clothes and adopting some of their other habits, the references were heard less often.

Konrad Lorenz is looked upon as the father of the modern science of ethology. As a result of his work, plus the work of many other diligent researchers both past and present, it appears that much of what is said and done in animal life is the result of common concerns such as territory, sex, or social standing. Sigmund Freud thought it was the animal in humans

46

*During the two hours I worked photographing him, this
bull moose constantly made guttural sounds to three others nearby.*

These hippos in South Africa are talking to one another.

rebelling against the pressures of society that created psychological problems for the individual. But it now appears that the same concerns and influences that confront humans are also the ones, if on a smaller and more simple scale, that confront most living creatures of the wild as well.

The sooner we understand these instinctive and psychological needs in other beings, the sooner we may understand the motivations that stir within ourselves and so be able to cope with them. The ability to recognize, first, that all orders of life have some form of communication with their own kind, and second, that we can benefit by learning to read and correctly interpret some of that communication, will make us, as individuals, more fulfilled and qualified for developing a belief in the oneness of life.

48

Chapter 3

The Role of Man in His Environment

Rudyard Kipling put it most appropriately in his classic poem:

> There was never a king like Solomon
> Not since the world began
> Yet Solomon talked to a butterfly
> As a man would talk to a man.

The Bible also talks of the wise King Solomon, son of David, who "spake with beasts, fowl, creeping things and fishes." Considerable evidence remains not only of early man's role in the environment but of his sense of responsibility toward it.

Unquestionably, primitive man was much closer to the animal world than we can imagine. That may be due to the status he imparted to other creatures. Ancient paintings like those in the Lascaux Cave depict magnificent animals, while the images of man bear a scrawny likeness. Could it be that primitive man, realizing the superiority of other creatures, worshipped the animals around him? And could it be that that same philosophy was carried down even to the native Americans, who also viewed all other creatures upon the land and sea with great respect? It seems logical. While man in ancient times may not have striven to achieve great things intellectually, physical prowess was crucial. Survival depended on physical ability.

Much of the evidence left in cave paintings and carvings, if we study these intently and allow an open mind, may appropriately be interpreted as conveying admiration. The animal world at that time may indeed have been revered. To be sure, killing occurred, for primitive man had to kill in order to live. But what was his attitude toward the killing? Was it ever done for sport, as we so often do today? And what about the American Indian? Frequently, before the great hunts, there were vision quests and periods of meditation, as well as prayer sessions asking forgiveness from the Great Spirit for the need to take the life of another being.

Spirit. Oneness. Do we as a society understand anything at all about such things? Or is it only self with which we're concerned? After all, we have been called the "me first" generation. Yet we can become gravely concerned about an endangered species. The possibility that a particular form of life may disappear for all time from the face of the earth brings an outcry heard across the land. Indeed, with proper respect for other forms of life, there's little reason why any creature (with a few exceptions) should ever have reached the point of being placed on the endangered species list compiled by the U.S. Fish & Wildlife Service or the World Wildlife Fund. If we really respected life in whatever form we found it, it would never be necessary for any creature to be obliterated from the earth by man. We would not wantonly destroy the home of our neighbor. So why should we destroy the habitat of other creatures that live all around us?

The animals and plants not on the endangered species list are just as important as those we've placed upon that roster, but they have not yet been reduced to a critically small

50

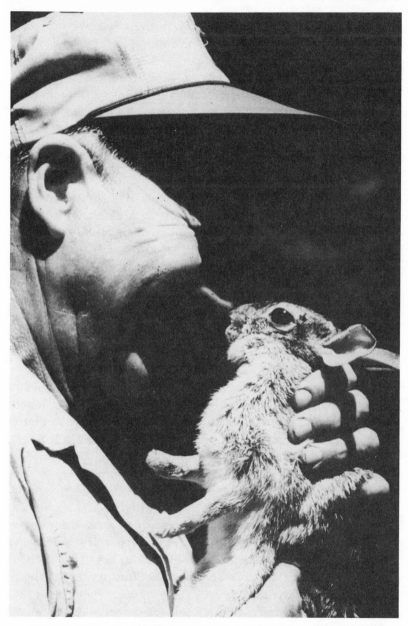

The late Lloyd Beesley, an Indiana farmer, talking with a cottontail rabbit he rescued from the mower.

number. They will, in time, simply because we live in a society that takes all and gives little or nothing in return.

For most of this century, perhaps spurred on by higher and higher degrees of technology, man has increasingly considered himself a spectator to what's happening in the natural world. Yet along with all the high technology has also come an awareness finally that humankind no longer can consider itself only in the audience. The great drama is one that concerns us all—each of us is carried along in the mainstream of consciousness.

Now and again I come into contact with whole communities of people whose wealth fairly exudes from the manicured streets. Multimillionaires' homes, with driveways sporting Ferrari, Mercedes, and Rolls-Royce automobiles, decorate the thoroughfares. From back of draped dens, their owners peer through iron-barred windows, alarm-controlled gates, at a world that is both foreign and dangerous. They have become insulated in their own cocoons. They have worked to accumulate wealth and, in so doing, have lost touch with reality. The basic source of their being is held at arm's length or beyond.

As humans, our number outranks all other species combined on the planet; yet because of our indolences we are far closer to extinction than many another species. We live on the brink of annihilation simply because we've created a world in which we need protection from one another. It's a world of luxury far beyond what we require to accommodate our own comfort or lifestyle. The margin of safety has been ignored within the world: We continue to place higher and higher demands upon the planet's natural resources until the day arrives when there will be no more. And what will we do then? Turn to synthetics? That's what we've been doing for decades now, only to find that more and more of those synthetics themselves hold health hazards which in time may wipe us out. Bent upon the course we've chosen for ourselves, it is only a matter of time before—one way or another—we destroy ourselves.

Nature has proven time and again that when a species

Bengal tiger, whose habitat is disappearing.

becomes overpowering and detrimental to life, its ability to correct the inequities diminishes and finally disappears. Everything in the animal world has a predator. Man, considered at the apex of the cyclic chain of life, was preyed upon by one of the smallest creatures in the chain: bacteria. Modern medical advances and technology have virtually decimated the predator, paradoxically breaking the cycle that could have saved the human race.

Balance—the ages have proven beyond question—is a vital provision of nature. Ruins of past civilizations attest to the rise of powerful people who then paid the ultimate price for their ignorance of a basic law of nature.

For thousands of years, man has searched in vain for a lost Eden, the paradise that perhaps was no more, in essence, than a state of mind. And still the quest continues, much of it now centered upon material things that bring only greater responsibility and concern rather than the esoteric happiness we so desperately seek. And yet, that evasive Eden may be all around us, overlooked by our own short-sightedness. If and when we are able to shed the shackles of selfishness, strip ourselves down to the humility of basic life forms, establish and differentiate our needs from our wants and desires, only then may we begin to discover the paradise intended for mankind from the outset.

Surely we now realize that everything, not only within our universe but in the entire cosmos, is interrelated. I was amused and amazed when I was working on a natural history book on American rivers a few years ago to see how much a network of streams resembles the labyrinth of vein and artery structure within our own bodies . . . and how much the rivers and their tributaries play the same role, sustaining the soil with life, carrying away the spoils, and renewing the land through which they flow.

And then, years later, when studying the formation of many of the off-shore barrier islands of North America, I was further impressed by their correlation to so many other aspects of the land and sea. It has been said that there is a definite, inexplicable relationship between the tiniest grain of sand

and the farthest star. I believe that analogy to be a simple and basic truth, one which we should not—cannot—ever ignore. We are part of the land and the water, the oceans and the stars, and all in between, for we are, whether we choose to recognize it or not, a oneness of spirit with all else that exists.

When we talk to animals, do we talk to them as King Solomon did? Do we treat them as equals, entitled to life just as much as we're entitled to life? Or do we talk down to them, treating them as inferior subjects that live to benefit our own existence? To communicate with or even understand other living creatures in the wild, we must first understand ourselves, learning to exercise such qualities as empathy and humility. For too long, we've been about the business of reaping the rewards from nature without contributing anything in return. Our society encourages us to nurture pride and superiority. We become so self-centered and self-serving that we grow obnoxious not only to those around us but to our own inner being. We are led to believe we must separate ourselves from the natural environment in order to exercise our dominion over plants and animals. There is no place or room for compassion, no time to look at the finer points of life, nor even to think about our own relationship to our environment. Too much, too often, we assume a macho attitude that insulates us from the very basics that support our being.

Naturalist tracker Tom Brown, Jr., in his book *A Field Guide to Tracking and Nature Observation,* has thought about such matters: "The values of pride and separateness are deeply woven into the fabric of our society, and they are not easily challenged or uprooted." Brown advises against trying to attack these values or tear them out. "That would only give them more power. As with any mental habit, it is best to change slowly and gently, nudging in a new direction without being too judgmental." He recommends as an antidote a long stay in the wilderness and talking to the animals.

But we live in an increasingly urban society. Most of us who express care and feeling for the wilderness and its creatures are, at best, only occasional visitors. Years ago, I made a feeble stab at moving from the city to the wilds, building a

Do these prairie dogs in Kansas value their lives as much as you value yours?

rustic house in the woods a mile back from the highway. It was an intrepid attempt to sample a bit of what goes on away from the rush and pressure of everyday society, an effort to step out of the mainstream and observe the flow of humanity. Since that time, I've hungered to live deeper in the wilds, to find a place where the horizons are not broken by another dwelling or the simplest indicator of man. Unfortunately, such places are almost nonexistent. I remember once listening to ecologist Dr. Eugene Odum, founder of the Institute of Ecology at the University of Georgia, speaking at a gathering at Duke University. "Wilderness no longer exists," he said. "Not in any form anywhere. When we have a world infiltrated by such problems as chemical pollution, acid rain, streams from which one can no longer drink, woods that have been mostly cut over, not once but several times, where more and more thousands of acres succumb to asphalt every day of every year—wilderness is a thing of the past."

Sadly, Dr. Odum's remarks are all too true. If I attempted to move deeper into my own little island of wilderness, I would only find myself moving out again on the other side. Even as I write this book, my house is closed to the sounds of nature. It is winter—the thermometer hovers near zero—and the sounds I hear are those of nature recorded, running water in a brook, the song of a Carolina wren and a distant warbler, the stroke of a canoe paddle on a northern stream, and finally, the forlorn song of a loon on some starlit northern lake. I have transported a facsimile of nature into my study; it is only a symbol.

From somewhere in my ancestry, Indian blood flows in my veins, and with it an eternal longing for the spirit of oneness. The native Americans called it the "great mystery," and they searched eternally for it. The early native Americans often spoke of other creatures as their brothers. They thought of them as just that, for they knew full well the value of life in whatever form. They realized that embodied in every living thing was the universal cause, the substance, the intelligence, the understanding. And they realized that their own lives must keep pace and be attuned to the same rhythm as the cosmos—the cosmos expressed in every living thing.

A few years back, one of my students presented me with a little book that appeared insignificant enough but would in time contribute much to my life. It was called *Kinship with All Life,* by J. Allen Boone, a Hollywood movie script writer and producer who was a direct descendant of Daniel Boone. That little book offered many intriguing relationships experienced by Boone with such creatures as Strongheart, the first canine movie star, and even Freddie the fly. But it also embodied the notion that one must deal with other creatures on an equal level if one is to communicate with them. Moreover, every creature on earth—and perhaps most plants as well—has something to teach us. But we cannot learn, of course, from

Would you treat this smiling alligator in the Everglades with respect?

any teacher unless we first of all know how to listen. And to listen effectively, we must place ourselves on the same wavelength as the teacher (not looking down our noses as we're prone to do with other forms of life) and open our minds and hearts to what is being said, or conveyed.

Boone once surprised a group of psychologists at a California university during a lecture when he tried to convey the idea of two-way thought traffic. "Man usually speaks down to the lower animals," he said. "We say, here I am up here with a big brain, and down there you are with a little brain. What can you send up to me? Even a common domestic housefly has something of value to share with you—whenever you are ready for the experience." If you have the "big brain" atti-

58

tude, there's very little you can learn from other forms of life. Your heart and mind are not open, and any information that comes your way is like water poured on a duck's back. It sheds right off. It's absolutely no different from any other form of learning. Close your mind, and you learn nothing; open your mind, and the knowledge of all time will flow through it.

Ivan Tors, the director of such filmed productions as *Flipper, Gentle Ben, Daktari,* and a host of others on television, draws a notable conclusion in an autobiographical work he calls *My Life in the Wild*:

> My conclusion, after a lifetime of research and study and after having been skeptic for some 20 to 30 years, is that we exist on a single conscious level and on multiple sub-conscious levels. Our conscious level is only the tip of the iceberg. Four-fifths of our life forces are not visible to us or to others, but they constitute our essence, our race, our memories, our cosmic connections, our belief systems, our feelings and premonitions.

Tors goes on to say that he believes we are interconnected with each other, with each living thing, with everything that exists in the cosmos yesterday, today, and tomorrow, and that love is one of the forces that connects us all. Love exists just as gravity or magnetism does . . . it can pass through time and space.

Allowing ourselves to communicate with other forms of life is perhaps the biggest and most difficult hurdle we face. In the first place, we cannot possibly perceive the meaning of life without knowing ourselves. To know ourselves is to know oneness, for that is the most basic ingredient of existence, of being.

During the course of gathering research for this book, I went to the California home of writer-naturalist Robert Franklin Leslie, author of *The Bears and I* and a number of other impressive works. Leslie and I talked an entire afternoon, and would have talked for an entire week, probably nonstop, except for my own pressing schedule, on our experiences with the animal world.

"It is not probable that most people will ever learn to talk to the animals," he said, "simply because they cannot identify with them. They have no understanding, feel nothing in common, and therefore, as they would be with another person with whom they felt no identical interests, are at a loss for something to say. I have never met an animal with whom I had no identity, nor from whom I could not learn something," he added.

Perhaps, I thought, after leaving Bob Leslie's home that autumn day, it is because we've lost the ability to communicate with other forms of life that we as a society experience so much difficulty communicating with one another. If we hold no respect for other forms of life, how can we have any understanding of oneness? And without sensing the oneness of the universe, we cannot possibly tolerate, much less understand other peoples, not only in our land but in foreign parts of the world.

There is not the least doubt in my mind now that the praying mantis, the wily fox, the light-footed prancing deer, the stately elk, the lumbersome elephant, and you the reader are all linked to the same roots, burned somewhere deep in the millennia. As a spider spins its web, we are connected in some fashion to a singular cell of life. We share the same ancestry and, somehow, the same unforeseeable future.

Petting a wild adult gray whale in Baja California.

Chapter 4

The Role of the Hunter

On a remote hillside in the southern Indiana county where I live is a crude but very unusual monument. It's a memorial to the last native whitetail deer killed in the county. The year was 1897, and the hunter, Rapp Pane, drew a picture of the big buck and inscribed the story and date of the killing. No deer had been seen in this part of the country for several years; they were believed to be extinct in the county. But Pane, while hunting squirrel that autumn, had spotted the buck and downed it. He thought it the last deer and stenciled in stone his pride at taking it.

The monument of the stone deer reminds me of a story that the philosopher-author Loren Eiseley mentions in *The Unexpected Universe*, about a poacher he had met in an English pub. The poacher said: "If there was only one fox in the world and I could kill him, I would do so."

Man the hunter is one thing. Taking the last of a species, regardless of the situation, is quite another. At what stage during the ages man began to play God is not known, but it is a misconception that seems to be growing upon our society. When tracking America's Sasquatch in the Pacific Northwest—a creature that, if it exists at all, is believed by some to be a vital missing link in the evolution of man—I began wondering what might happen if man indeed did succeed in meeting up with the legendary Bigfoot. Would it be photographed, studied as much as it would allow, and then permitted to go it's way, to live it's life as it has done for thousands of years? Or would it be captured, taken alive if possible, dead if necessary, even if it were the last surviving member of it's species? More than likely, it would be killed.

Since primordial time, man has traditionally been a hunter. His world was filled with animals physically his equal if not his superior. To protect himself, to ensure that he himself did not become lunch for another creature, he had to kill. To feed himself, he also had to kill. For thousands of years man remained a hunter simply to ensure his own mortality.

At what point man began to hold the animals in his environment in high esteem, to look upon them as more than merely a source of food or a predator, is not made clear in documented history. One would suspect it did not occur overnight, nor even within the span of one lifetime, but over a period of thousands of years. By the time cave artists started to depict animals some 15,000 to 20,000 years ago, they had already begun to learn from the world of beasts. There are some indications that man was beginning to incorporate the creatures of the wild into his religion even before leaving Africa.

Thousands of years passed, however, before history was to record definitely man's worship of the animal world. Engravings of gods—half man, half beast—were prevalent in the ancient Egyptian culture, dating from 3400 B.C., and later in the Greek, Roman, and even the Mayan culture in central America. Ironically, it is probable that creatures of the wild have never been held in lower esteem than during the nineteenth and twentieth centuries.

The religious role of animals infiltrated into the North

Man has traditionally been a hunter.

American continent through tribes which brought their phi-
losophies with them from Asia over the Bering Sea land
bridge that once connected the continents. It is still seen to
this day in the totem poles carved from trees by the native
peoples of the Pacific Northwest. The American Indian living
in what is today the lower forty eight contiguous states and in
Central and South America certainly incorporated the animal
world into his own religious beliefs, a practice that diminished
upon the arrival of the European settler and missionary.

By the time America was discovered, hunting as a way of
life in Europe had long given way to agricultural pursuits. The
plow and the shepherd had brought about vast changes in lifestyle: the status of animals declined simply because survival
no longer depended entirely upon them. As man domesticated
animals, however, it was still necessary to communicate with
them. Farmers needed to know how to manage their charges;
but to do so, they needed to develop an understanding of
them.

Herdsmen enlisted the help of domesticated wolves—
dogs—to tend their flocks of sheep and cattle. Exploiting the
wolf's natural hunting behavior, they recruited pairs of dogs to
work as though sheep or cattle were deer or caribou. The dogs
stalked or circled them, crouched if the animals became too
alarmed and, if necessary, jumped at their throats to turn the
leaders and control the herd. To watch a good sheepdog tend
it's flock today is to watch a highly trained inbred descendant
of the wolf.

On the North American continent, however, the hunting
ethic still prevailed. Yet the native American, like the ancient
Egyptian, continued to revere animals. Wild creatures were
his brothers, his intermediary for communing with nature and
with his deity. He considered the various traits of animals, and
each tribe adopted its favorites according to how admirable it
considered those traits. For some tribes, the wolf was the celebrated animal spirit, for others the bear, for others again the
eagle or the bison. The animals held in highest esteem often
were the same animals most avidly hunted.

Before the European, the native American had achieved

a high level of harmony with his environment. He was close to the land and all that lived in or upon it. Because of his great understanding of and concern for his fellow creatures, the highest degree of conservation practice normally was followed. When there were hunts, the animals killed were totally used in one way or another. The meat was eaten. Entrails were used for the storage of food or as sinew for sewing. The hides provided clothing and shelter, and horns and bones were fashioned into tools or ornaments. Even the dried dung fueled fires or fertilized the few crops tended by the women and children. Absolutely nothing was wasted. To waste was a grievous sin.

Therefore, Indian culture taught the hunter to take only what was needed. No indiscriminate killing was permitted. And as important as the hunt itself was getting to know and understand one's prey. The hunter must be fully aware of the animal he would slay—its virtues, strengths and weaknesses, the very essence of its being. In the course of getting to know the animal, he came to admire it, to create stories similar to those of ancient times from the Old World (such as Aesop's *Fables*), and to develop a brotherhood with the creatures of the wild kingdom. It was the same way with birds and fish. The following prayer by a Kitsumkalum Indian in British Columbia expresses the relationship between a fisherman and a salmon:

"Welcome, swimmer, I thank you because I am still alive at this season when you came back to our good place; for the reason why you came is that we may play together with my fishing tackle. Now you go home and tell your friends that you had good luck on account of your coming here, and that they shall come with their wealth, that I may get some of your wealth."

Whenever the Indian went hunting or fishing, he did so with reverence in his heart and soul for the quarry he was about to take. He did so with mixed emotions: sorrow for the life he must extinguish; joy for the meat and hides he would bring home to comfort and nourish his body and those of his fellow tribesmen. When he took life, he did so only because it was necessary for his own survival.

Until the Europeans came to America, there was no other

Some Native American tribes celebrated animal spirits such as the eagle's.

reason to kill animals. But with the advent of trading, when the whites convinced the Indians they needed such things as guns, knives, trinkets, and jewelry (although the Indians had been doing just fine without them for hundreds upon hundreds of years), the native Americans turned against their brothers of the wild. They no longer took only what they needed for sustenance. Now, they took as much as they could for trading. Hides and meat were in demand by the whites, and in return, the Indian could have all the comforts and pleasures the European offered. The purpose of hunting changed almost overnight. And so did the custom. No longer was the hunt a reverential occasion. Instead, animals by the thousands were sought out and slaughtered for the new, demanding market.

What the whites could get from the Indians was still not enough. Wild game was everywhere, and the greed of the whites gnawed at the herds and colonies like devouring dragons. Commercial hunting operation were established as trails became roads and railroads, giant steel ribbons that unfurled across the land. And, of course, the pioneer settlers depended almost entirely upon the wildlife for their own needs. A hunter and his family might easily kill several dozen larger game animals and several hundred smaller animals during a single year. Buffalo Bill Cody earned his nickname by slaughtering more than 4,200 bison during an eighteen-month period to supply the needs of railroad construction laborers in 1868–69.

The mood of the country was to conquer the wilderness, convert the land by the plow, settle the landscape from horizon to horizon. There was absolutely no concern for the wild creatures or for the American Indians who had lived upon the land for an eternity. Politicians in Washington felt that if the animals were all slaughtered, it would help subdue the Indian, bend that culture to the white man's will. And it worked. By the time the Buffalo Bill Cody era had ended, the American bison was all but eliminated. Most of the deer had been wiped out. So had the elk, moose, bear, and more than half of the antelope. The land was being conquered, the Indians were virtually starved out, and the animals were all but gone. Not only had the white settlers conquered the land; they had created, as far as the wilderness and wildlife habitat were concerned, a vast wasteland.

Only during this century has any real concern been expressed for wilderness, for wildlife, and for conservation. Although there were a few wise spokesmen such as Thoreau, John Muir, and some of the Indian chiefs like Seattle of the Duwamish and Joseph of the Nez Percé who warned of a day of reckoning, anyone lesser known who advocated communing with animals risked being committed to the nearest insane asylum. Only during the past few decades has the idea of sharing with all living things become more acceptable in our society.

Paleothic man hunted out of necessity; so did the early American Indian as well as the European settler. But why do some 20 million Americans, twenty-one out of every one hundred men and two out of every one hundred women, hunt today? The U.S. Fish & Wildlife Service of the Department of the Interior, the chief agency for wildlife management in this country, periodically conducts a survey that attempts to reveal the real reasons.

Most hunters do not really know why they hunt, but many will tell you it's because they enjoy it. Beyond that, they're lost for an explanation. Perhaps it's some ancient instinct burning deep within them that drives them to hunt, even when there no longer is any real need. Some will say it's because hunting is a public service to wild animals, that by hunting they prune the herd so none of the remaining animals will starve to death. They seem to forget that before there was a white man to prune the herd, even before there was an American Indian, most species survived quite well. Of course, there were predators then—the big cats, wolves, and bear. Those have mostly been removed now, so hunters can point out with glee that indeed there are more deer today than there ever were before. But what about the rest of the animals? Certainly there aren't more panthers today than ever before, nor bobcats, nor wolves. Those have all but disappeared. Why not bring back the predators and expand the habitat?

69

Bighorn desert sheep, an endangered species, in Arizona.

Some hunters are interested in collecting trophies.

Unquestionably there's a need for predators, but can man, in addition to playing God, also fulfill that role? Most wildlife experts think not. Man, they say, is not even fulfilling the role of predator with respect to whitetail deer, which is, along with the rabbit, the most hunted animal in America. Why? Because the natural predator does more than simply keep the numbers of animals in check. It chooses the weak, the sick, the crippled, and those animals that are nearing old age, and so doing, it improves both the herd and the species. Man, the hunter, makes no such distinctions, nor is he in a position to do so. Many times he takes the finest animals in the herd. Man's discrepancy leaves much to be desired, so when the hunter presents this argument in his defense, he simply is not aware of the role nature plays in taking care of her own.

71

Two writers—John Madson and Edward Kozicky—once described hunting as "a complex affair with roots too deep to be pulled and examined. If a hunter is asked to explain his sport, he can no more rationalize hunting than he can describe emotion."

In 1973, Stephen Kellert, a staff member of the Yale School of Forestry and Environmental Studies in New Haven, Connecticut, conducted a study on attitudes towards animals, domestic as well as wild. From that study, he was able to construct seven stereotypes connected with hunting, based on people from all parts of the nation:

1. The person who is strongly attracted to wildlife and the outdoors.
2. One who favors habitat over creatures, and goes hunting to sample the atmosphere.
3. Humanistic types who tend to personify all animals.
4. Moral persons who stand on ethical principles against killing.
5. Utilitarians who view animals only insofar as they benefit humans.
6. Religious types who look to the Book of Genesis which preaches man's dominion over the earth and all that lives on it.
7. The negative person who is fearful, superstitious or indifferent toward animals.

Of the three basic hunting types also defined by Kellert, the meat hunter showed up with the highest percentages in his survey. Nearly half of those 20 million hunters claim they do it for the meat; yet when one figures the cost involved, an average of between $5 and $10 per pound for dressed-out wild animals, the economics are missing. And it's certainly not convenient.

Kellert's behavioral research shows that the second largest group of men and women hunt for what they call "sport." Sport means they kill for fun, to answer a challenge within themselves, for amusement. The sport hunter is most apt to be the good conservationist. He hunts for sport, but he also hunts to conserve.

John Mitchell, author of a series entitled "Bitter Harvest" that ran in *Audubon Magazine* back in 1979–80 and examined the pros and cons of hunting, defines conservation in the hunter's terminology as "the wise use of natural resources. It is," he added ironically, "growing trees in order to chop them down. It is chopping them down in order to grow deer. It is growing deer in order to shoot them down. It is shooting them down in order to spare them a ghastly death. And it is paying special fees and excise tax that, according to the National Shooting Sports Foundation of Riverside, Connecticut, in large part have 'kept America as green as it is today.'"

The third group—the lower percentile of the three—is the nature hunter, the person who goes hunting but doesn't care whether he kills anything or not. It's just being out there that counts. Hunting is merely an excuse to be outdoors, and the guns or archery outfits simply provide a rationale. They could do just as well with cameras and long lens and come back with more trophies without taking a solitary life.

The sport hunter, besides being the conservationist, also comprises that group of monied individuals who travel the world in quest of the so-called Big Five. They're the trophy hunters and couldn't care less about the meat; in many cases, the animal's carcass is left lying where it falls. The Big Five are considered by those ego-serving individuals who hunt them to be the most dangerous big game in the world: lion, leopard, rhinoceros, Cape buffalo, and elephant. The principal legacy, aside from rows of dusty, disembodied heads and the depletion of many species all over the world, is the alienation many urbanized people feel for wild animals. Fact is, unless provoked, no species of wild animal is dangerous, and all will go out of their way to avoid contact with people. But the stories manufactured by big game hunters make the animal seem the villain and the hunter who slays him the benefactor of humanity.

Neither the big game hunter nor the sport hunter in general will get very high marks as a communicator with wildlife.

Tracking in winter presents a challenge.

Nor will the meat hunter, for this is the category in which most of the so-called slob hunters are found. They want to kill to take home something to eat. Poachers also fall into this category, and there are plenty of them around, particularly when the ecomony takes a nose-dive and dollars for buying meat at the supermarket are harder to come by. Others kill to eat not because they need to, but simply because there's some deep-down voice within them that challenges them to hunt and to kill.

The nature hunter may indeed establish rapport with wild animals. This person is the one most likely to get buck fever and be unable to shoot an animal, even though he has one lined up in his sights and needs only pull the trigger. Many never pull the trigger and, after a few seasons of hunting, may hang up their gear and do all their hunting with cameras or binoculars for the rest of their lives.

Hunting has some positive roles, too. Without question, there are more whitetail deer in America today—about 12 million—than there were when Christopher Columbus dropped anchor in the Caribbean in 1492, and hunters are partially responsible for that. Through their purchase of licenses, they contribute tax monies to support high-intensity game management programs which provide, among other things, additional whitetail deer habitats. And were it not for Ducks Unlimited and that organization's impressive effort in creating extensive waterfowl habitats, there would be far fewer waterfowl in North America today than ever. In some states, such as Indiana, the proceeds from hunting license sales have also been extended to the management of non-game species.

So hunting can—and does—play a role in our environment; and it certainly has an impact upon many creatures of the wild, as well as upon those of us who attempt to communicate with and build a greater understanding of the animal world.

Unfortunately, hunting has many other negative aspects as well. Beside the fact that plenty of people are turned off by the killing of wild animals (*Audubon Magazine*, just by running Mitchell's treatise on hunting, lost many subscribers),

75

some hunting atrocities consistently occur, which cast it in a distasteful light in the eyes of landowners, farmers, and ranchers.

Years ago I posted the land I own around my house, simply because I did not wish anyone to hunt there. As a nature photographer, I find many of my subjects close to home. For more than two decades, I've tried to build a greater rapport with the creatures that live around me, especially woodcock, grouse, and whitetail deer. And yet invariably some hunter will come to my door to ask permission to hunt. I appreciate their asking, for it gives me a chance to explain my position. But within two weeks after two men had asked to hunt and had been politely refused, I chanced to meet them again less than two hundred yards from my house—on my property— early one morning stalking deer.

A few years ago, one of my teenage sons approached four men with dogs who had ventured onto my property hunting rabbits. He explained to them that we allowed no hunting and showed them the posted signs. He was chuckling when he returned. I asked him why and he shook his head in disbelief. "Three of them were state conservation officers," he said. Up until that time, he had expressed an interest in becoming a conservation officer himself, but he never mentioned it again.

After graduation and a year in the U.S. Forest Service, my son joined the Army. The last time he was home, we discussed the turn of events in his life. "I'm still sort of a conservation officer," he said. "I've become a highly trained hunter of men. If I'm ever required to hunt, it will be to preserve a way of life."

His expressions reminded me of a story I read in high school English class. It was called *The Most Dangerous Game*, by Richard Connell—and I shall never forget it. Connell depicts the plight of Rainsford, a sailor washed ashore on a remote Caribbean island to become the quarry and sport of the lone resident, General Zaroff, a world-renowned hunter who has grown bored with hunting big game and has turned instead to hunting humans. This provides a far greater challenge for him. In the end, the wily Rainsford, using many tricks he

My son David on his first and last hunt.

has learned in hunting from natives all over the world, wins out and the hunter becomes the hunted. The story left an indelible impression in my mind of what an animal must experience when he is hunted by armed men with dogs.

Nevertheless, I was at one time a hunter. Indeed, I grew up hunting. Like so many others, I relished the taste of wild game, and every fall and winter we had wild meat on the table at least once a week. As I grew older and had children of my own, I tried to impress upon them the need to hunt. None of them ever wanted to do so, but I remember well talking my oldest son, David, into going hunting with me. He carried a small .410 guage shotgun, and we went hunting for cottontail rabbit on my father's farm in Kentucky. Tromping through broomsage where I suspected rabbits were nestled, he suddenly jumped a cottontail. I waited for him to aim and fire. "Get it!" I shouted. He was ten years old at the time. As he pointed the gun, blue smoke belched from the nozzle and the rabbit went tumbling end over end. We both walked to where it lay, and as we approached, the rabbit, bleeding from its wounds, kicked straight up, then flopped spasmodically around on the ground.

"You have to shoot it again," I said. "It wasn't a clean kill." He shuddered, and tears streamed down his face as he brought the gun to his shoulder and fired. The rabbit lay limp on the ground. David is now in his mid-twenties, and to this day, he has never again gone hunting. I doubt that he ever will. I never persuaded any of my other sons or daughters to try. A few years later—in 1970, I think it was—I did my final hunting story, a piece for *Field & Stream Magazine* on hunting swamp rabbits on islands in the Mississippi River. Entitled "The Plight of the Swampers," it called attention to an animal whose population was swiftly being depleted.

Since that time, I've continued to hunt, but I do it with a camera instead of a gun. I find the challenge far more difficult but the rewards much greater. I am thankful I once hunted with a gun, that I killed. It taught me the value of life and made me respect other creatures to a far greater degree than I would have done otherwise.

*Some hunters travel the world in search of the so-called
Big Five—one of which is the elephant.*

I remember Tom Brown, Jr., talking of killing his first
deer. It was a small buck, and Brown, who is an expert on
wilderness survival and tracking, armed only with a hunting
knife, dropped from a tree onto the deer's back, thrusting the
knife into its throat. "The deer wouldn't die," he said. "It held
onto its life with unbelievable tenacity, bucking, kicking, and
straining to get me off its back. Finally, I was forced to choke
the life out of it with my bare hands."

"That was a powerful experience for me," he went on,
"for I became part of the deer's final struggle. I saw the hor-
rified look in its eyes and felt its spirit slip through my fingers.
That deer's death brought me closer to the essence of life than
I had ever been before, and it taught me a grave lesson. I will
always remember that taking an animal's life is very serious
and can only be justified with real need. And secondly, should
that need exist, one must take every precaution to avoid in-
flicting needless pain and suffering."

I learned much from hunting that has contributed since to
my understanding and respect of wildlife. And many of the
techniques I acquired then have been most useful in my pursuit of nature photography. The experiences I enjoyed while

79

hunting were indeed lacking when compared to those challenges and experiences I have had with a camera and through observing the creatures around me. But because I was once a hunter, I can now go into the wilderness with some knowledge of both the hunter and the hunted. I am glad of that experience.

Chapter 5

Learning to See

To work successfully with creatures of the wild means to know them, to understand them, and in some cases, to establish some degree of rapport. What, for instance, is the porcupine really like? How does it feel, where does it live, what does it like to eat? Does it feed at night, as many animals do, moving about the forest during the hours of darkness and sleeping during the day? Do porcupines talk or otherwise communicate with each other? Or with other wildlife species?

Each animal species bears distinct differences, of course. And within a species each individual is different as well. Although every species may be considered in general terms, those of us who have worked closely with creatures of the wild kingdom know individualism plays as great a role here as in our own society. The sooner we can fully understand and accept this fact, the greater our chances of being successful not only in working with creatures, but in understanding their actions and hence communicating with them.

I am convinced, based upon my own experiences, that one can learn more about the wild kingdom through observation than by any other means. Not always is it an easy task.

This red fox is alert and wary but curious about me.

While some animals, birds, or reptiles are easily observed once we place ourselves in their domain, others are rarely seen, even though they may live or move about very close to us. The bobcat, raccoon, opossum, and many other creatures do virtually all their feeding as well as other activities under cover of darkness. Many of these creatures, particularly the raccoon and opossum, live not only in the open countryside but also within the city. They often feed upon the contents of the family garbage can; yet unless they inadvertently knock off the lid with a great clanging sound, you may never know they are there until the following morning when you find litter strewn about your driveway. So knowing something about animal feeding habits may be very important in your observation efforts.

Secondly, learn to recognize the marks animals leave. Tracking is a highly challenging and skillful art, but once you have grasped it, just being able to read the different tracks of animals will tell you much about what goes on in their world and what they're like. Learn to recognize and identify scat or droppings. In some cases, animals use their excretions to identify the boundaries of their established domain. This may or may not be important to your quest, but if you can identify scat, you may be able to determine what kinds of wildlife are present within a given area of terrain.

Last, learn something about the mating habits of the animals you wish to know. Sex and food play a paramount role in the lives of all creatures. Discover when and where they mate, when and where they feed, what kind of tracks they leave behind, including droppings, and you will have fulfilled the prerequisites for becoming an integral part of the wild kingdom you're about to enter. The most important learning process, however, is achieved through observation, and, having once observed, accurately interpreting what one sees.

Being in touch with your immediate environment has much to do with your success in observing or noticing what goes on about you. I've been in the woods with folks who saw exactly the same things I saw, but failed to notice them. The fact that something most interesting is occurring right before their very eyes somehow fails to register. Why? Their thoughts are not attuned to their surroundings. Their minds are miles away, thinking about something totally removed from their present environment. For many people, going into the wilds is an almost useless experience. They might as well stay home, for they have carried with them all of the world they are burdened with at home. If their minds are perplexed with problems in their business or social world, they bring that with them to the wilds, and by so doing, they insulate themselves against the natural environment around them. Consequently, it's necessary to package your problems and all the trivia of the everyday world, and leave them at home. Tell yourself there's plenty of time to work on them when you return; for now, you're going into the wilds. By so doing, you unburden the mind and alert the senses for the more immediate things you may experience.

Generally speaking, we observe with our eyes, but observation is not done with the eyes alone. So many contributing roles are played by other senses that help us see better—and to understand what we are seeing—that it's difficult to separate them. But for simplicity, we'll try to limit our discussion here mainly to observing—the art of seeing. And not just seeing, but recognizing and recording, interpreting what we see. One of the greatest challenges I face in the nature photojournalism seminars I teach across America each year lies in teaching my students not just to look, but really to see. There is a great difference. Developing an eye is a tough assignment that comes only with much effort and considerable experience in the wilds.

The "wilds" here can mean any area that smacks even remotely of being natural. It can be a park, a woodland, a meadow or farmer's field, a stream or lake or pond—any place where the presence of man is diminished and the world of natural occurrences is increasingly predominant. Once you learn to see in the wilds, you'll be able better to appreciate life wherever you live, work, or travel. And you'll become more conscious of all that moves or exists about you. Your life, in essence, will become wealthier.

The whitetail fawn's spots are camouflage in the dappled forest understory.

If you know a veteran woodsman, associate with him. You'll learn much during a single outing. If you don't, strive to train yourself. A basic step is to look about you. Don't attempt at first to pick out details, but look at the broad general landscape. Scan the horizon. Look behind you as well as ahead of you. Look up, especially if you're in a wooded area. As many creatures live in the trees as on the ground. If you come to water, first look at the water itself—the total expanse of it, as much as you can see. Only after you've percieved the overall environment and recorded the shape, texture, and color of it— some of the elements that make up it's character—should you begin to look for detail.

A good training exercise in developing the powers of observation, especially during your initial sojourns in the wilds, is to plug your ears with cottonballs. You will thus be forced to rely on your sight. Soon you will come to notice the most seemingly insignificant movement. You spot the texture of bark upon the tree. You may notice a particular dead tree, and how it's been drilled full of holes by a woodpecker. Or there may be even tinier holes, placed there by an insect or worm. You see movement in the trees. It's a bluejay, one of the protectors of the forest. He's come not only to observe you (as you are the observer) but to send out the alarm to all the other creatures of the forest. It may or may not be his intent to alert the other residents of his world that you are here, a stranger in their midst, but he does it out of habit. The crow is the same way. They are among the first to note your presence and to let it be known by their calls to all others within earshot.

Because of this alarm, other creatures may react in some particular fashion. Most will go about their business, knowing full well you are there. Some may run and hide until they ascertain whether you are harmless. And others may, out of curiosity, come to see you, to observe you from their secluded places. It is my belief that your presence will not only be known, but it will also be noted whether or not you carry a gun, particularly in an area frequented by hunters. If you do carry a gun, the message sent will be different from that conveyed if you are unarmed and pose no potential threat.

I decided it was to my advantage when working with wildlife to go both unarmed and in a receptive and friendly state of mind. I also had earlier decided it would be greatly to my advantage to learn all I could at my local library about any specific creatures I wanted to observe or photograph. Fortified with that knowledge, I would be better equipped to achieve success. Just another way of saying that one should, when one goes into the wilds to observe wildlife, give oneself every advantage possible.

Being able to observe and develop a relationship with creatures of the wild is most often a lonely experience. You'll see much more if you travel alone or, at most, with only one other person. The more aware the second person is of your mission, the more successful you'll be. Too often when two people share an experience, their senses are too much directed toward each other, either consciously or subconsciously, to allow the necessary attention to the natural environment about them. Consequently, much that goes on escapes their observation.

I've gone walking with another person on a beach, for instance, who walked completely through—stepped upon—exceedingly delicate patterns created in the sand by the winds during the previous night. In one case, on Padre Island off the coast of Texas, the carvings were so delicate, varied, and interesting, I could have based an entire photo essay on the artistry of the wind. But one footstep by my partner annihilated the entire creation.

Another time, I went on an outing with a local Audubon Society group into a proposed wilderness area of the Hoosier National Forest. More than two hundred people gathered in their automobiles on a gentle autumn day, an ideal time to be sharing an experience in the hickory-oak-poplar forest. The outing included a three-mile hike into the woods, across hill, valley, flowing brooks, and up rocky ravines. The hike was more or less single file, but soon people began pairing up or

87

This mother moose in Alaska charged at first but later paid me no heed.

walking abreast in little groups, stopping here and there to talk among themselves, and then moving on when the group leaders were ready for them to do so.

During the entire afternoon, I heard virtually no comment from a single person about the area itself, about the rock formations, the general lay of the land, although I'm sure there must have been some such discussion somewhere along the way by somebody beyond the outing leaders. My wife and I had taken two of our youngest children along—both boys, one eleven and the other five—for we wanted them to have this experience also. When we returned to the roadside parking area, our younger son somehow had disappeared. A wildlife artist friend and I retraced our steps into the woods to find him. The area where we had been was a disaster. It looked as though a small herd of pachyderms had traveled this way, not a well-meaning group of nature lovers from the local Audubon Society.

We later found our son with another group of people who had shared the experience. But the fact that I had had to retrace our steps left me with an unforgetable view of the forest, minus people, through which we had traveled. It was appalling to see the evidence of what we had left behind; moreover, it would take the woods a year or so to recover from that singular outing.

But I dare say, the worst of it was that probably not more than half a dozen hikers benefited greatly from the experience. It was my impression that few of them were even aware of where they had been because they were so intently involved in conversations with their neighbors or friends. For all they learned, they could just as well have stayed home. Certainly they didn't see any wildlife, for any wild creatures living in that entire tract of woodland knew very well of the visitors' intrusion into their domain. And they would know about it for a long, long time.

Once you've entered the habitat of wild creatures, there are two basic methods of observation. One is to move quietly and easily through the area, pausing here and there to look about you, up as well as down, and certainly behind you. The other is a method popularized years ago by the intrepid Brit-

Knowing how high in a tree a bird likes to perch is an aid to spotting it. I photographed this ptarmigan in Alaska.

ish naturalist Ernest Thompson Seton: Enter the habitat, find a suitable spot which allows you an excellent field of vision, and sit or stand completely still and silent for hours on end. This gives the natural world about you time to accept your presence and, because you're not moving or showing any sign of life, to gain confidence in going about the natural course of events. Henry Thoreau practiced this method at Walden, and later wrote about it. I've tried both methods—use them periodically from time to time still—and find both work to varying degrees.

Once while employing the Seton method in my own Hoosier woodland, a gray fox came galloping through the forest. I could hear it coming before I saw it. I was sitting on a slope, tilted toward the morning sun, with my back against a white oak tree. From this vantage point, I could see a good fifty to sixty feet and more than one hundred degrees from side to side. My ears told me the running sound was a dog, but then a fox appeared on an adjacent ridge, loped easily down the ridge, leaped across a ravine, and came up the slope almost directly to me. Since there was a light breeze blowing into my face, the fox was not able to detect my presence by smell. But within a dozen yards, its keen eyes saw me and the animal stopped dead. It knew I didn't belong there. Though I had a camera nestled in my lap, I dared not move. The camera was cocked, however, and since I had a wide-angle lens on it, I knew I could get a picture from its present position without worrying about focusing. The great depth of field of this lens would automatically allow me to get a good picture. Still, I did not move, except for an occasional blink of the eyes.

The fox didn't know what to make of this. So after studying me intently, it once again opened its mouth to breathe, its tongue hanging loosely. I knew I had at least gained some of its trust. Then it turned its head away, looking from side to side all about. Apparently it did not see anything else it questioned within view. Next it turned briefly aside, walking around me in one direction, then turning and walking in the other, always keeping me within peripheral view. I knew if I

Even large animals, such as this blond grizzly bear in the Toklat Valley of Alaska, can be hard to see unless you are alert.

so much as moved a single muscle, this beautiful creature would be off in a jiffy.

Still, curiosity was bearing down heavily. I could sense it well, and I knew it was only a matter of time before the fox would either come forward or decide to ignore my presence and be on its way. Curiosity won out, and after stopping to study me two or three more times, it edged cautiously forward. By this time I had edged my finger to the shutter release of the camera and as the fox stood not more than eight feet away from me, I slowly and methodically squeezed the

92

trigger. The sound was like the report of a rifle breaking the silence of the forest. The animal leapt back, crouched for a split second, and then was off, bounding through the trees the way it had come.

The thought crossed my mind many times afterward what might have occurred had I not had a camera, had I sat perfectly still and allowed this magnificent animal to continue its approach. How far would it have come? And what would it have done?

Being a good observer takes much patience. Moving through the natural habitat is precarious business. One should make every effort to blend into the environment. Just as some people are offended by certain colors, there is reason to believe that animals feel the same way. Keep in mind that many creatures are color-blind; they see only in black and white, or varying tones of gray. Others, including most birds and many species of insects, see in color, but their color array may be quite different from our own. Because of the variety of animals and/or birds you may be observing, it's perhaps best to consider some form of camouflage. That means wearing clothes that blend with the environment, clothes that are not offensive in odor or sight or sound. Earth colors—green, brown, sometimes sky blue—are generally acceptable. During hunting season, however, you should wear bright yellow or blaze orange just to keep from getting shot. You should also consider the texture of your clothing for its non-glare and sound-producing qualities. Woolens and buckskins are quiet fabrics; cotton and synthetics make too much noise. Exposed hands and face often give away an observer. You can wear light gloves to cover the hands, but a facial covering may not be feasible. Charcoal or grease smeared on the face, just to break up the lines, will work well. Make sure, though, that whatever you use is odor-free, or if not, that it's permeated with natural odors of the wilds.

Also learn to flex your body. Bend to go under overhanging limbs rather than bulldozing your way through them. When I was a lad on my father's Kentucky hill farm, I considered it a challenge to travel through wild blackberry patches as quietly as possible and without a single scratch. Even though the briars presented what appeared to be an almost impenetrable barrier, I delighted in attempting to work my way through these thickets, sliding around and through the briars and emerging fifty feet away on the other side without a single prick or scratch. I learned patience this way. One could not rush through a blackberry thicket. Neither does one rush through wildlife habitat and expect to see wild creatures.

Years later, when I had become a commissioned officer in the Army's Intelligence Corps, I utilized the same methods to lead reconnaissance patrols into enemy territory, past posted sentries, to gain the information I was sent to obtain and retreat without being detected. To be successful in a life-and-death situation like this requires much attention to detail and much patience. There cannot be a single mistake, a single giveaway. To be successful at observing wildlife requires just as much attention to detail, just as much patience.

By taking your time, stopping often, and looking carefully all about, you're able to detect movement. It's the nature of many animals to freeze when they realize there's a stranger in their midst. And since they're already, in most instances, camouflaged by their natural environment, you likely won't be able to see them until they move again. Being able to detect movement is a definite prerequisite to observing wildlife.

Once you've located a specific creature you wish to observe, make sure you're downwind, that is, the wind is blowing from the creature being observed in your direction, not from you directly toward the creature. Most wild animals have a keen sense of smell and can not only detect your odor but to some degree analyze it. Because of pheromones—those external chemical secretions which researchers believe to be dead giveaways to what you're feeling inside—the animal may be able to sense not just your presense but your intentions. And since most creatures live in a state of survival, most likely they'll not wait around to judge if they've read you correctly.

Try to remain obscure while you're observing a specific subject. If that isn't possible, at least try not to alarm it. If you wish to move closer, do so with great caution. Do not move

Beaver are spotted more easily by their wake in the water than they are spotted on land.

toward the creature when it is obviously watching you. Wait until it returns to grazing or whatever else it was doing when you first saw it. Then move slowly and deliberately toward it. I never move directly toward any creature, but if at all possible at an angle to it, much as you would do if you were tacking a sailboat into the wind. Upon reaching one point of the tack, turn back in the other direction. The object of this is to let the animal think you're interested in something else in the vicinity and are actually going to move past it en route to someplace else. I use this technique in photography a great deal, and it nearly always works. Periodically, I stop to observe and take a picture, but only when the animal is obviously paying no attention to me. In this way I've been able to get remarkably close without spooking my subject. If the animal becomes alarmed and shows signs of getting nervous, I pause, freeze, and wait until it seems more at ease again. Although I keep my face pointed in the direction in which I'm going, I have the animal almost constantly under surveillance out of the corner of my eye.

It's necessary to keep close visual contact with the creature being observed. Only then can you read all the signs: the flicker of the ears in the case of deer or elk, the look in the eyes, or the attentiveness to whatever it is doing. Once in Alaska, while working with a cow moose, mother of small twin calves, I tried to read every movement as I stalked closer and closer. Although I use high-powered telephoto equipment, I like to use only smaller telephoto lenses, working closer and closer to my subject.

When I came too close, Mama Moose laid back her ears and I could see the fire mounting in her eyes. I knew she was going to charge any moment, and she did. Several times during the three days I lived in close proximity to her, she charged me, chasing me through groves of trees. But the charge was short-lived each time. And each time I was able not only to outdistance her but to maneuver more quickly than she could around trees. Her object, of course, was to tell me that she considered me a threat to her calves and didn't want me working that close. My object was to get good photo-

Animals like this prairie dog are easier to spot in motion, but keep your eye on them once they freeze or they'll "melt" into the background.

97

graphs of the moose family lifestyle. The calves were totally unconcerned and unafraid. And as the time passed, the mother became less concerned, too, for she learned I posed no threat and meant no harm.

Working with some animals, you might use a blind. National wildlife refuges sometimes establish blinds at spots frequently visited by animals or birds; others will permit you to set up a portable blind for wildlife studies. If you own a tract of your own land, you might like to build a permanent blind and bait an area periodically by placing food or, in the case of hooved animals, a salt block nearby. Over a period of time, animals will come there to feed or lick the salt, allowing you to observe them from the blind.

A blind doesn't have to be anything fancy. Mainly, it's any object, left in place so the wild creatures become accustomed to it, that will provide a wall between you and the creature being observed. It also hides the person behind the blind, of course, allowing a peekhole through which to observe activity in the natural world. In many cases, creatures are well aware that the blind is occupied, but they feel confident simply because there's a barrier between the observer and themselves.

A blind can consist of natural materials procured from the area, such as bunches of sedge, sticks, tree branches, leaves, mud, all erected so as to hide the observer from view. It can also be old canvas, an old tent through the sides of which have been cut some small peekholes, a building (preferably made from natural wood), or a made-to-order blind purchased through a sporting goods store. Depending upon what types of wildlife are being observed, some photographer friends of mine have even dug foxholes in the ground deep enough for them to stand in and peek over the edge.

Several things are absolutely necessary in a blind. It must be large enough to permit free movement; it must be comfortable; it must fit in with the natural surroundings; it must provide seclusion; and it must allow a good field of view. The blind should be located downwind, so that prevailing winds do not carry your scent to the animals being observed. Of course,

When animals interact with each other, like this pelican trying to push away a gull, they are often too intent to notice your approach.

99

this is not always possible, but your blind will work much better if you're able to achieve this end result.

Sometimes blinds can take very unlikely forms. Naturalist-author Edwin Way Teale kept swinging hammocks set up at various locations on his Connecticut farm, where he could spend hours lying out in the woods observing what went on about him. Very often, animals would move about nearby simply because they were accustomed to seeing the hammock there all the time. When I was working with sandhill cranes a few years back at a state game area in northern Indiana, I used an old piece of tarp, which I spread on the ground and weighted down at the corners with field stones to keep it in place. I did this several weeks before planning to use it. And even though the game area provided elevated observation towers, which also serve as good blinds, I was better able to work lying prone under the old tarp with my head sticking out from under one edge. I could manipulate the cameras just fine from this position and quite often was able to work with the shy sandhills less than fifty feet away.

An automobile also makes a good blind if you use it on a road normally used by cars. I've observed and worked closely with deer, bear, elk, antelope, and moose from inside my vehicle, with the window rolled down. If I get out, however, the entire situation changes, and the animals usually spook quite quickly.

Of all the virtues of successful animal observation, patience is the greatest. Patience and careful study of the terrain around you. The woods may be full of deer, but you may not see them at all until you have stopped, studied intently, time and again, letting your eyes rove slowly over the view before you. Sometimes, it's almost as though the creatures grow right out of the forest, evolving into view—and yet they may not have moved at all. They were there all the while, but it takes time and patience to allow your eyes to see what's before you. Many an inexperienced hunter has passed right through an area literally crawling with deer and not seen a single one . . . something I imagine must give great delight to the creatures of the wild.

100

Daylight is not the only time to wildlife-watch. Dawn and dusk are excellent, and even after dark is good.

I've come to believe many wild creatures enjoy observing people almost as much as we enjoy observing them. Often when I'm out in open terrain, hawks or eagles will fly overhead, wheeling above me not once but several times, apparently interested in what I'm doing there and watching my movements. A few years ago while pursuing caribou in Alaska, I found it impractical to continue the chase. I didn't seem to be getting any closer to them; the further I pursued them, the further away they ran. The area happened to be a dry, braided riverbed with many channels cut by snow melt during the spring. It was now autumn, and water flowed only in some of the channels. The dry ones often were three feet deep. As my assistant and I gave chase, we came suddenly upon one of the dry stream channels and promptly dropped into it, lying prone.

We lay there for five minutes. Finally, I peeked out to see what the caribou were doing. Every one of them had stopped and was looking back quizzically. They couldn't figure out what had happened so suddenly to their pusuers. I knew curiosity would soon get the better of them. I was tempted, as I'd heard of some deer hunter doing, to tie my handkerchief on a stick and wave it in the air, but I didn't. Periodically, I peeked out to see what the caribou were doing. A couple of animals soon turned back, then others joined them, coming back along the same route they had gone, getting ever closer.

It was only a matter of minutes before they would be upon us, and just at the right second, I leaped up and got off six shots at close range before the startled animals bounded away. It was not only fun, but a successful way to get pictures. The startled look on the faces of the caribou was precious; I shall never forget it.

There is little doubt in my mind that members of the wild kingdom are indeed as interested in observing us, the members of humankind, as we are in observing them. They just don't make a practice of it, as we do; they don't have to. There are always more than ample numbers of humans around to watch. Only it may be a little tougher for them to analyze what we're doing, or why.

Bison—these are in South Dakota—often allow a close approach.

Chapter 6

Learning to Walk and Stalk

$\mathbf{B}$y the time most of us have reached the age of two, we've learned to make the necessary coordinated motions that will propel us, on our own two feet, from one location to another. Upon achieving that skill, it's generally said we've learned to walk. If we're to become proficient in our associations with wildlife, however, we often must perfect skills of movement we never before thought possible.

Older generations of American Indians could run across dried leaves in a deciduous forest without making a single sound. John Muir, father of the Sierra Club, once voiced amazement when he looked up from his campfire in the high Sierra Range to find an Indian standing not three feet away, gazing at him. He had not heard a solitary sound. But native Americans spent great time and effort learning to move quietly through all types of terrain; they became skilled at the art of walking.

The proper way to walk in the woods may be quite different from the way you're walking now. Take out a pair of your old shoes and study the soles and heels. Where are the worn places? That should tell you a great deal about the way you've been walking.

Learn to walk quietly. Learn to sensitize your feet. To walk quietly and develop sensitivities for feeling the earth, you should place your foot down lightly as you walk. The outside ball of the foot should touch the ground first, then roll slightly inward letting your toes feel the earth as you settle your weight down on that foot. Imagine your foot as the rocker of a chair, and practice rolling your step from front to rear and back again. Keep the toes slightly lifted. They, like the fingers of your hand, are for the feelings, not for bearing the weight of your body. Never should you place the heel down first, yet many people do exactly that—digging in, pounding the ground or concrete pavement on which they walk. Walking should be a smooth, harmonious exercise, a movement that is poetry to all parts of the body. By learning to feel the terrain on which you're walking, you'll learn to move more quietly and easily.

How well you walk and how quietly is going to depend somewhat on the type of shoes you wear, too. Soft shoes are best, yet most outdoorsmen and backpackers, hikers and bird watchers wear those terrible cleated clods the manufacturers would have you believe are made for the outdoors. They are, if you don't want to experience anything on a trip except getting there and back. If you want to develop sensitivity, wear thin-soled shoes through which you can feel the ground you walk upon. I once met an expert bus driver in Michigan who wanted to take me for a drive in a new bus he had just purchased. When he entered the door, he took off his shoes and drove in his stocking feet.

"Why did you remove your shoes?" I asked.

"So I can feel the engine and the road and be in tune with both," he replied. "Through my stocking feet, I can feel anything unusual the engine is experiencing. I can also feel the tires on the road. It's my way of being in tune with and part of this bus."

The same is true of being in tune with the land on which

A red fox in the Alaska interior was so intent on stalking a ground squirrel it failed to notice me—even when I was an arm reach away.

you walk. The American Indian wore moccasins because they were lightweight, protected his feet, and most importantly, afforded a rapport with the land. To be successful as a wildlife observer, it is essential that you become in tune with the land. It's actually best if you can go barefoot, but unless you're already accustomed to this, it may take months to toughen your feet enough to go into the wilds with no shoes.

Learn to feel with your toes. Notice, too, with your eyes where you're stepping. Remember, you must learn to see in all directions—that means on the ground, as well as down the trail and overhead. So cultivate careful looking. Be aware of what you're stepping on. If it's something that's going to make noise, such as a brittle twig or stick, avoid it.

Sometime when you're walking in the snow in an isolated place where you can study your own trail, note the angle of your feet at the time they made the track. Many people allow their feet to protrude outwardly at the toe. The toes should be straight ahead of the heel, pointing forward, not at an angle. In this manner, as the foot is swung forward, it takes up less space and is less likely to catch on another object, especially in close understory or brush. Movement, once you've trained your feet in this way, comes with less effort; the blending has begun. When you've practiced this art for a few weeks, you'll find your feet learning to see, to touch, and to know and understand. They become contiguous with the earth on which you walk.

When my three sons were young, we used to play a game in the woods. I'd place them about a hundred feet apart and then walk some three hundred yards away and stand facing a tree. Upon signal, they were to sneak through the woods, seeing which one could get to me first without my hearing them. It was weeks before they learned to move quietly through a deciduous forest. But they learned their lesson well, and it's something they'll never forget, either.

There were other times during winter snows when we'd hike into the woods and they'd track me. Giving me a fifteen minute headstart, they'd then work out the trail. It was not easy, for I would deliberately double-back, cross my own trail

107

Students learning to stalk at Tom Brown's Wilderness Survival & Tracking School in New Jersey.

at numerous places, walk backward in my own footprints, walk in a small brook that flowed through the woods, climb trees, walk on logs and, like the foxes I knew during my childhood, use all the imaginative tricks I could muster. But only a few times did they fail to find me. Sometimes it took a good half day or more to decipher my trail in our thirty-acre woodland, but they would work it out among themselves. Before we began our game each time, I reminded them I didn't want to hear *them* walking, either. So they learned not only to track, but to be quiet about it. After they felt they were getting pretty good at tracking in the snow, we tried the same woodland in the spring when there was no snow and the going was a bit tougher. It was a great learning experience for my sons and great fun for all of us as well.

To make you more aware of how noisy walking can be, start listening to others. Rarely will you meet a single person whom you cannot easily hear. You'll soon become more and more aware of how you yourself walk and will most likely make a more conscious effort to walk in a different manner, one that is quiet.

Another good way to teach your feet to see is to use a blindfold. By walking through a familiar place without the aid of sight, you automatically learn to feel with your feet. Once you get past the initial stage of anxiety, you will find yourself settling down, becoming more relaxed and more sensitive to those parts of your body that can help you to feel your way along. Try walking with a blindfold for just ten minutes the first day, then twenty the next, and finally a half hour. Once you fell comfortable with a half hour, you may extend your practice session to an hour, depending upon how much time your schedule will allow and whether you have familiar terrain in which you can walk safely.

Learning to walk properly—and quietly—is a basic exercise in getting to know the wildlife about you. It will allow you to get close without being observed or, if you are discovered, to be accepted as part of the natural environment. Walking, of course, is but a first step. After you've learned to walk, you should learn to stalk.

109

Stalking is merely another form of walking. The pace slows down; the body is lowered into almost a crouching position. Movement is light and deliberate. If you've ever seen a common housecat stalking a songbird, you'll get some idea of how you should go about stalking. The cat crouches low, keeping its eyes upon its quarry. It steps forward lightly, one foot at a time, placing that foot in just the right position before putting any weight on it. Then it eases forward . . . very slowly and deliberately. The entire stalking movement is beautiful to watch. There are no finer stalkers on the planet than members of the cat family. I've seen tigers and lions stalking big game, cougars and bobcat sneaking up on smaller animals. The intensity of the stalk, the beautiful poetic movement, are the same with all cats.

Many times the cats are unsuccessful. I remember observing a mountain lion in the Chisos Mountains of Big Bend National Park, in Texas, stalking two mule deer grazing at the edge of a meadow. The lion made its way very carefully down an incline punctuated with rock outcroppings, being careful to use the rocks for cover. The closer it got to its quarry, the slower it went, and when nearly eye-level with the deer, it dropped into a full stalking posture, its stomach almost touching the ground. The ears were bent forward, the tail straight back, the yellowish-green eyes staring intently, almost hypnotically, at the deer. Every muscle was at the ready, but the big cat seemed relaxed and able to respond at a moment's notice. I watched as the animal drew ever closer, expecting it to bound forward and strike down an unsuspecting deer at any time.

Just then, a hawk soaring overhead shrieked, and one deer lifted his head. As it did so, it must have caught a glimpse of the crouched mountain lion. Snorting, it bounded off in the other direction, and the second deer followed in hot pursuit. The lion kept its position, watching them go, but I can imagine what must have been going through its mind at that moment. Then, disgusted, it rose, turned, and walked away, looking back once or twice over its shoulder.

110

Using good stalking techniques led me to within a few feet of this brown pelican, which shows no fear.

111

When you're stalking your way closer to animals, keep in mind this story; it's important to your ego to remember that the greatest stalkers on earth sometimes fail. Then perhaps you won't be overly disappointed if your efforts sometimes come to naught. Watching the mountain lion that day made me a better observer, and certainly improved my own stalking endeavors.

Veteran tracker Tom Brown, Jr., claims that by using expert stalking methods, he has actually sneaked up on grazing whitetail deer and touched them. He says he has done this several times without the animal being aware he is about. That's because he utilizes the natural cover around him, because he possesses the skill to walk and/or stalk quietly, and because he blends with his surroundings and is able to freeze his movements whenever the animal looks in his direction.

Again, this takes much practice, patience, and time. It can be done, but as Brown points out, you must be as one with the animal being stalked. One must understand the quarry completely, know what its likely to do and when, and share a special closeness with it. Without this affinity, Brown says, one cannot hope ever to achieve the ability to stalk to within arm's reach of another animal in the wild.

It's best not to begin practicing on a whitetail deer. Although deer lack far-sighted vision, they have other highly developed senses and spook easily. Start by stalking smaller animals. When I was a teenager, I was able to get within a shadow's length of cottontail rabbits, so close that if I fell I would have crushed them. I've achieved the same success with squirrels feeding on the ground. Rabbits or squirrels work well for your practice sessions, but frogs or snakes are even easier. Then try it with butterflies. They're really tough to stalk.

Once when I was working on my book *The Swamp* in the Big Thicket of eastern Texas, I teamed up for a couple of days with photographer Dan Guravich, who was involved in another project. One day, we noticed a bush literally covered with monarch butterflies and decided we both wanted to get pictures. Dan slipped around on the back side of the bush, a good ten feet away, and I was going to work from the front side. We would move inward alternately, closer and closer. The butterflies right away noticed we were there, and as we inched closer, they became jittery and flushed, disappearing in every direction. Some landed on a bush fifty feet away.

Cautiously, Dan and I followed. Again the butterflies moved on to yet another bush. Again we followed. Soon we had chased them more than a quarter of a mile through the swamp, with no success at all. Suddenly, I realized what we were doing and broke into a laugh. Dan looked at me quizzically. "These butterflies," I said chuckling, "are just leading us deeper and deeper into the swamp. And we're not getting any pictures." Dan looked at his watch. "Yep," he agreed. "Do you know we've been chasing these butterflies for nearly two hours now?" We both stood laughing, and the butterflies went on their way.

Since then I've stalked butterflies many times and have experienced a great deal more success, first, because I did it more slowly, and second, I think, because I was alone. Butterflies are naturally more skittish about two people than one. But always, when it comes to stalking them, butterflies have been challenging.

Stalking can be great fun. One of the keenest satisfactions I can remember in my whole life was another type of stalking—past alert sentries during my military career. At that time, it was necessary to do more than assume a crouching position; I had to go to a crawl. It was in a field of knee-high weeds, and there was no other cover, but by crawling I could be largely out of sight. The position will work in some instances with wildlife, too, and is especially useful on beaches, in meadows, and in other treeless areas with poor cover. By going to a belly crawl, you not only have a low profile, but you're close enough to the land to be a part of it. You begin to notice other things as you move along: to smell odors and to see many of the smaller creatures, insects and spiders and worms, that live close to the earth. Be aware, but don't be distracted from your quarry.

Keep your toes straight, so they don't catch on any other

Stalking can result in great closeups such as these of muskox, Nuvinak Island, Alaska.

114

objects. Bear your weight upon your knees and elbows, using your hands to feel your way, or part the vegetation so you make less noise as you move forward. A crawling position does not work well going downhill. But it works extremely well going upgrade or on more or less level terrain. Punctuate your crawl with periodic pauses, raise your head slowly, methodically, looking about you. Then crawl forward again with your head tucked down, low enough that you don't break the line of vision above the tops of the weeds.

The crawl is not always justified, but it can be a very beneficial way to move about at times. Just remember, you learned to crawl before you learned to walk. Many animals live close to the earth; that way, they're much more a part of it. After you've had a few crawling sessions, you, too, will become more acclimated to the earth and most likely will develop a different point of view. It can be very rewarding.

There are no schools to teach you how to walk or crawl or stalk, although Tom Brown's Wilderness Survival & Tracking School in New Jersey comes closer to it than any place else. Mainly, it's something you're going to have to teach yourself. And you do so by learning to know yourself, looking inwardly to the person you are inside and paying attention to the way you yourself do things. Become aware of the way you walk. Notice how you carry yourself, how you move, whether you possess any poetry at all in those motions. You can do certain exercises, of course. Running upstairs, two at a time, and later, three at a time, will help. Do it without lurching. Going into a park or refuge—anyplace that will get you off pavement and onto the good Mother Earth—will allow you to listen to yourself walk. Can you hear yourself? If you can, then you need to work on the skill of walking. It won't come easily, nor overnight, but with enough practice it can be done.

And then a good exercise is to stand on one leg, raising the other leg as high as you can get it, straight out and fully extended. Then swing that leg straight out behind you. Learning to balance is very important. Learn to step lightly on the outside ball of your foot, then roll it inward until you've placed the weight squarely on that foot. Step highly and deliberately,

115

but do everything in slow motion, paying attention to where all parts of you are at any given moment. Then imagine you've been spotted by an animal you're stalking. You must learn to freeze (stand dead still) at any moment, regardless of position, and to hold that position for up to ten minutes. Can you do it? If you can't, you need more practice.

Situps, pushups, and deep knee bends are good conditioning exercises, too. But you should do them for fifteen to twenty minutes every day until you've achieved some degree of stability and toughened your muscles. You'd be surprised how much such exercises will condition and tone up your muscles in just two weeks' time.

Another good exercise is one I learned from Tom Brown himself while attending his school a few years ago. It's called the weasel walk, and it's done by crouching in a position barely elevated from a squatting position: the knees bent; the back, head, and eyes straight forward; arms hanging closely at your sides. Walk quietly this way for a hundred yards. The next day, try two hundred yards. Increase the distance a bit each day. The first couple of days will nearly kill you, particularly if you're out of condition, but you'll gradually get more accustomed to it. Your muscles will begin to tone up, and the soreness will soon leave. The weasel walk is an excellent conditioner, and you may wish to use it periodically in the wilds when stalking animals.

You will find these exercises beneficial not only for tracking or stalking wild animals but also for your health. They will build your body and at the same time provide you with an exciting new activity. But your education has barely begun.

When animals are preoccupied with feeding, they often allow close approach, like this bull moose in Montana.

117

Chapter 7

Reading Signs

To understand the creatures with whom we share our planet, we have to know how to observe and interpret their actions; but we also have to learn to read the signs they leave in their own natural environment. Everything that moves about upon the earth leaves an imprint. If it eats, unmistakable signs indicate what was eaten, and how and when. A bent twig or sprig of grass can indicate direction of travel. Scat (droppings) can tell something about a specific animal's diet. In the case of grazers, the shape of the scat may indicate the time of year the animal passed this way, even though the observation might be made months or even seasons later.

By learning to read signs, we may also determine the population density of creature habitat and how active those creatures are at the present time in their movements. Correct reading of signs can be of paramount importance in leading you to prime locations for observation. Tracking and reading signs are fascinating sciences and pastimes in their own right. A good woodsman is by nature a good sign reader. The early American Indians were, too, though today, sadly, most of them have lost the art.

118

The wilds are full of signs. They're not as brazen as the signs lining our highways, of course, but once you learn to look for them, they are just as apparent. Like road signs, they point the way, inform, and sometimes relate complete dramas that have occurred. The more you look, the more you see. The art of tracking and reading signs is to me the most challenging element of learning woodsmanship and successful observation. The more you study signs, the more you realize that all things in nature are in some way interconnected and interrelated.

Of course, you don't have to become an expert in reading signs to enjoy an association with wild creatures, but it certainly helps to have a working basic knowledge. Tom Brown, Jr., says he considers being able to read signs as the "icing on the cake" for any outdoor experience.

Brown, who learned his art from an old Apache during his growing up years, has published a series of books on the subjects. He probably is America's best-known professional tracker. Another good guide that will help you identify animal tracks is the *Peterson Field Guide to Animal Tracks,* by Olaus J. Murie (published by Houghton Mifflin in Boston).

A good way to start studying signs, of course, is by merely identifying tracks. Once you've introduced yourself to tracking, you may then begin to study other signs like droppings or scat. And beyond track identification, learn to interpret what the creature was doing at the time it made the tracks. Learning to identify tracks is the simplest part of the entire sign-reading task. The identification guidebook can help you here. From that point on, it's largely a matter of memorizing their shape, size, and appearance. Remember, though, that the perfect footprint rarely exists in the wild, so you must learn to read and identify the imperfect print. Tracks of a rabbit, for instance, may appear quite differently in snow than they do on sand or in wet mud. The tracks of most creatures also differ somewhat when they are running full out as compared to when they are leisurely walking.

Wild animals, of course, are shy and in most cases naturally try to avoid contact with humans. A large number are nocturnal, feeding by night and sleeping in burrows or se-

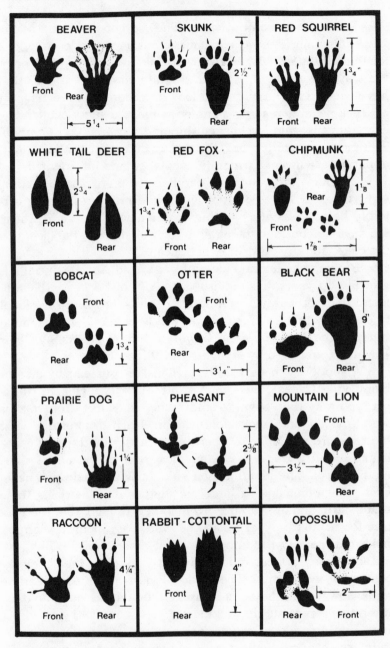

Common animal tracks.

cluded spots by day. We may rarely see the larger population of the wilds, simply because we aren't likely to be there at the time creatures are moving about. But if we're capable of reading signs, we can certainly determine, first, whether they were there, and second, what they were doing during the dark hours of the night.

When learning to identify and study tracks, it's best to work along streams or around ponds or lakes, places that have soft mud shorelines. By checking early in the day, you'll be able to discover something about what occurred during the night. Chances are good you'll see raccoon tracks—they often follow the water's edge in their hunting quest. You may also see mink, muskrat, beaver, otter, skunk, or opossum in such places, depending on what part of the world you're in. This is a particularly good way to begin your studies simply because soft wet mud tracks are apt to be more perfect than those found in other terrain conditions.

A handy device for assisting you here is a simple tracking stick. You can make it easily from virtually any kind of tree limb you find in the fields or woods. It should be straight, lightweight, and about four feet long. Next, wrap four rubber bands at different places along the length of the stick.

Now, say you're tracking a deer. You find a couple of well-defined prints in soft ground, but the trail then leads onto hard ground or among some pine needles and leaves where it's difficult to detect. Laying the stick on the ground near the easily visible prints, place the rubber band at one end of the stick so it's lined up with the deer's heel. Then position another rubber band opposite the toe of the next step. The distance between these two rubber bands indicates the length of the deer's stride, or the distance between steps. Now turn the stick sideways and adjust the remaining two rubber bands so that they measure the width of one of the tracks. Place the stick next to the last print you see, pointing it in the same direction the deer was heading, and you'll know where the next print should be. Get down on your hands and knees, and search the ground carefully. There should be some indication, although ever so slight, that the animal passed this way. Continue to use the stick this way, moving from footstep to footstep. The stick will help you through some difficult places, and as you become more proficient, you'll be able to track an animal even across solid rock, using only a tracking stick and a sharp eye.

Once you begin to achieve some success at identifying tracks in the mud, you may then move away from watering holes into the woodland or onto sand or snow. These will certainly give you more challenge. You may have to get down on your knees or stomach to study the tracks (Tom Brown calls it "dirt time"), particularly when you begin "aging" them. Tracks are aged by the crumble rate of the mud or dirt around their edges. The perimeter of dirt surrounding the track is also important; by studying it, you often may be able to tell what the animal that made that track was doing at the time. Bulges at the front of the track may mean the animal was bounding or running full out, thereby creating pressure ahead of the tracks as its feet landed on the ground. Professional trackers call these pressure ridges, and they tell much about the creature that made them.

Studying animal behavior through the signs or tracks they leave is a most intimate experience. It takes much patience and attention to detail. Bent or broken grasses largely go unnoticed by the average person, but to the tracker, they're important. Tom Brown, Jr., having spent years perfecting his skills, claims he could track a deer halfway across the country, across solid rock, sand, grassland, mountain, stream, and lake. But it would take months to do so, and by the time he was a few miles down the road, the trail would already have grown so cold it would be next to impossible to follow.

All my life, I've noticed animal tracks. Having grown up in the country, there were always plenty of tracks around to study, and I spent a fair amount of my childhood doing just that. I studied snake tracks that led across country dirt roads near my home. I got to the point where I could almost tell the size of the snake not only from the breadth of the track but by the curves of its twisting path. I tracked box turtles, frogs, raccoons, and rabbits. There were no deer in my part of the

Reading tracks in soft earth is the best way to begin.

123

country then, but there were cows, horses, pigs, and chickens, and I studied those tracks as well.

The most challenging experience in my career as a nature photographer and observer of wildlife, however, came years later when I picked up some magazine assignments to track the legendary Bigfoot or Sasquatch in the Pacific Northwest. Several of my children, along with my wife, were also interested in participating in that assignment, and so in the spring, just after school was out, we hitched our camper to the family station wagon and headed for British Columbia. For the better part of that summer, we stayed on the trail of the Sasquatch, interviewing all kinds of folks in Canada, Washington, Oregon, and western Montana who claimed to have had encounters with this possible missing link in the chain of evolution. Between interviews, we searched the landscape. It was along a creekbed in the vicinity of Mount St. Helens (later to make worldwide news when it erupted) that we first came cross some footprints we believed had been made by this huge apelike creature the American Indians called Sasquatch. The prints led up the streambed, which was nearly dry, toward the mountain. The U.S. Forest Service had earlier told us there were reports of Sasquatch activity in the area, but no one really believed it. We were not sure, either, but we did make some plaster-of-Paris casts of the prints, which we kept for several years.

We trailed the tracks that day as far as we could, until they no longer were legible and finally, as dark approached, left the area. Again the next day we were back, and for several days thereafter, but that's as close as we ever came to seeing Bigfoot in the wild. It's possible, of course, that some practical joker in the area had made the tracks. But many times since I've mused over that experience and wondered how it might have been had those tracks actually led us to a bona fide Sasquatch, which we could have photographed to prove to the world that such creatures do indeed exist. Unquestionably, this would have been the ultimate experience in animal observation.

Near the end of my hunting career in the early 1970s, I

Some animals leave very distinctive tracks.

had another tracking experience I shall never forget. I was photographing a story for *Field and Stream Magazine* on tracking and hunting bobcat with some expert bobcat hunters from Missouri. We rendezvoused at dawn on the Kentucky shore of the Mississippi River. My hunting companions brought along three highly trained and time-tested cat dogs. They were expert trackers, I was told. We traveled by boat to an 1,800-acre island in the midst of the stream, which area contacts claimed was heavily populated by bobcat. It was an ideal hunting situation. The dogs could track well, the weather was overcast and cool, for it was now early December, and it had rained the day before. The dogs, of course, would track by scent, not sight, but it was interesting to have accompanying tracks to follow, too.

I learned a great deal during the experience about tracking and about bobcat. For three days we tracked on the island, and although there were four well-experienced hunters in addition to myself and the three dogs, we never saw a single bobcat.

The tracks, some old, some fresh, were everywhere. The dogs picked up fresh trails to follow every few minutes. The cats were moving, no doubt, but they were keeping well ahead of us and out of sight. After the first half day, I decided they were playing a game with us. No one lived on the island, although farmers on the Missouri shore tended crops here. The cats were seldom hunted and in retrospect I believe they enjoyed the experience even more than we did.

The hounds would no sooner pick up one bobcat's trail to follow than another cat would cross that trail, leading the dogs in a new direction. It had happened numerous times during the three days we were there. The dogs were literally run to death—and so were the hunters trying to keep up with them. At night the first day, both men and dogs dropped into camp almost too exhausted to eat dinner. The second night was worse, and by mid-afternoon of the third day, we were all ready to give up the hunt to save our sanity. We left the island, defeated by a half dozen or so bobcats. Probably there were more bobcats on the islands, but we felt at least that

Raccoon tracks are among the most common and easy to find beside streams and lakes.

127

many had joined in the game with us during the time we were there.

Tracking can be a fun experience, as well as a rewarding one. I've followed the trails of both wild turkey and grouse in my own Indiana woodland. I had moved from the city to the hill country of southern Indiana ten years before I knew there were wild turkey on my place. One of my high-school-age sons once reported spotting a single gobbler in a wooded ravine two hundred yards from the house, but I felt he must be seeing things. Wild turkey had been stocked in the Hoosier National Forest twenty five miles to the south, but we'd never seen any in our neck of the woods.

The following winter, while hiking through the woods in fresh-fallen snow, I came across the largest chicken tracks I'd ever seen. "Turkey," I exclaimed half-aloud, although I was walking alone. I tracked on for a quarter mile before deciding it would be useless to go any farther. The turkey obviously was moving a lot faster than I was, and my chances of catching up with it before nightfall were indeed quite slim. The experience proved one thing in my mind, however—that my son's report of turkey in late summer apparently was right. He had seen a gobbler in our woods. This might or might not have been the same one. Where there's one turkey, chances are good there are several.

Winter is an interesting time in our woods. The first snows herald the beginning of tracking season. None of my family hunts to kill anymore, but all of us are much involved with the outdoors, with nature and with wildlife. We've posted our lands and try to protect the wild creatures that live there from hunters. We enjoy them too much in other ways to allow them to be killed. We try to develop relationships of trust with them, although we realize that may be dangerous for the animals themselves if hunters trespass—and they frequently do—on our lands.

As I've said, tracking is not only a challenge but great fun. And it's rewarding to know how many creatures of various species live within our woodland. We may never see them, yet we know they are there because we see their signs and their tracks, which show up particularly well in the snow. Grouse, woodcock, wild turkey, squirrel (both grays and the larger fox squirrels), raccoon, opossum, woodchuck, rabbit, red and gray fox, whitetail deer, skunk, shrews, wood mice, and numerous songbirds are our neighbors. A couple of times we've seen the tracks of bobcat, and once, the elusive animal itself.

Two years ago a pack of coyotes came to live in the woods, and for several months I periodically heard their distinctive yipping at dawn, but I've not heard them for some time now. Wild dogs were travelers through the area on a regular basis at one time, although I only saw them twice. I knew they were there by the tracks and signs they left, however. Knowing this may have spared me a bad experience one morning as I jogged down a trail through the woodland to a small lake where a group of mallards lived. I always like to end my jogs with a dip in the cool waters of the lake before breakfast. As I loped downgrade to the lake, I heard off to my left other runners—these had four feet—and I looked up just in time to see three large wild dogs charging directly toward me. Luckily, there happened to be a dead hickory sapling pole lying nearby. I quickly picked it up and faced the lead dog squarely, yelling as loudly and menacingly as I could.

The challenge stopped the dogs dead in their tracks. They stared momentarily and I stared back, right into their eyes, then shouted again and charged toward them, holding the pole with both hands like a javelin in the air. They turned tail immediately and disappeared into the understory. I haven't seen them again to this day. A month later, a neighbor reported that hunters had killed two of them. I suppose that was true, for I've not seen even their tracks in the woodland since that time.

Tracking is an ancient science. It was probably practiced to a far greater extent by prehistoric man than it is today simply because it was a skill necessary for survival. Many animals also track, but they do it by smelling the trail. Humans at one time may have been able to follow a trail by scent also, but if so, we have long since lost the art.

129

Bobcats are hard to find even when you've discovered tracks and other signs of their presence.

When I'm running in the morning, I'm often accompanied by my dog, who has a marvelous time running off in this direction or the other following her nose. I used to own a little long-haired dog named Bonnie who was a mix of beagle and cocker spaniel. Her background gave her a very sensitive nose. We would be running down a trail, virtually side by side, when suddenly she'd pick up a scent leading across the trail. Often it would stop her dead in her tracks, or she'd immediately turn to the left or right as though a barrier ahead had made her do so. I knew some creature had just been there, perhaps moments before, and had left a fresh trail for her to follow.

Bonnie could track very well, but that's all she could do. Those among us who have studied tracking even superficially know there's much more to tracking than just following a trail. Experienced woodsmen have learned to read imperfect track records with remarkable skill, just as a trained ornithologist recognizes a bird without seeing it. You can tally up a long list of birds if you go bird watching, but you're not likely to do that with animals. You must become a super sleuth to be a good animal observer, and tracking certainly will assist you in doing that.

Tracking or learning to read signs is no easy task. It does require you, as Tom Brown says, to put in a lot of dirt time. It's also more of a science than perhaps any other related field dealing with wildlife on an amateur basis. You learn to utilize so many different aspects of what you see. You look for not only tracks, but droppings, gnawings, scratchings, dams, nests, burrows, and rubbings. Several of my immature pine trees and some flexible hickories have become rubbing trees for deer. Periodically, I notice the bark rubbed from these trees hanging in strips. The deer have used them as we would use a back scratcher, and the bucks may have used them to rub the velvet from their new antlers.

When you find tracks in the field, particularly in mud of a consistency that you can handle, you may want to scoop up the track with a small spade and carry it home intact for further studies. Or you may wish to make a plaster-of-Paris cast that you can carry home and preserve for study. You could carry a

131

*Examining animal disturbance of vegetation is rewarding
but harder than following tracks.*

notepad and pencil with you for noting some of your observa-
tions. Or you could photograph the tracks to further study
later, or to share with your friends.

Whatever degree of interest you possess in the wild kingdom, you'll find learning to track and read signs will indeed
enrich your outdoor experience, giving new impetus and
added meaning to a great aesthetic adventure.

132

Chapter 8

Learning to Listen;
Developing a Sense
of Smell

Enriching our experience in the outdoor world means we must develop our sensitivities to a high degree in all areas. We hear only if we learn to listen. We smell much better than we listen, but many times we're unable to interpret what we smell. Being able to associate a scent with a particular creature or plant in the world of nature is very important. The outdoors is full of sound and odor; it is the reason dogs have such a grand time going for a walk in the woods or fields. They constantly are being barraged by scents which they wish to pursue. And so a dog, if you'll notice, is constantly dashing off the trail here and there, constantly sniffing the ground or the vegetation simply because it finds interesting odors there.

Seldom does a dog listen for sounds; instead, it relies

upon its nose to guide it to the source of those odors. But we humans do not have such highly developed olfactory sensors. We rely more upon sight and what we hear. Yet neither our hearing nor our sense of smell is nearly as highly developed as those of the animal world. Many of the sounds emitted by animals are ultrasonic, and either too high or too low for us to distinguish. A deer can hear our footsteps long before we are in sight. Even snakes hear, although they have no ears on the surface. Just how they hear so well is not fully known, but the hearing system is there. They also respond to vibrations, especially vibrations on the ground, which they pick up through the bone of the lower jaw.

Fish make sounds and talk to one another, although in tones audible only to themselves. This fact was discovered by the U.S. Navy during World War II, when acoustic mines on the Pacific coast began blowing up for no apparent reason at all. Studies later showed they were detonated by the sounds of fish calling to each other.

Fish also easily pick up vibrations. A few years ago when I was working on a book on the Ohio River Valley, I met a bartender in a river town who said he could call fish.

"I have a whole pond full of fish at my place," he said, "and I can call them to the bank where they'll take food from my hands."

Figuring this to be a typical bartender story, I was ready to dismiss the whole thing until I met a banker who knew the bartender. I asked him about the fish.

"Oh, yes," he swore, "it's for real."

A day later I was at the bartender's home watching him pat his hands lightly on the ground alongside the water and call to the fish. Pretty soon, I saw the water moving and fins close to the surface. Seconds later, a dozen or more largemouth bass had gathered to take food from the bartender's hands. Some of them practically came out on the bank to get it. Since the pond was at least a quarter-acre in size, I knew the fish had to be listening or they would not have heard. Or, if not listening, they certainly were good at picking up vibrations.

134

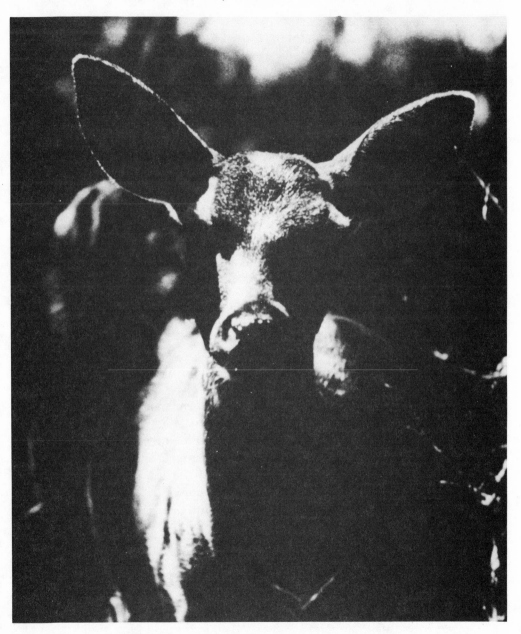

A deer can hear our footsteps long before we are in sight.
The tiny Florida Key deer is listening intently.

Although birds and animals make many sounds we can hear, some of their sounds are too high or too low for us to distinguish.

Several years later, I met Ranger John Halas at Florida's John Pennekamp State Park, one of the nation's few underwater parks, who had experienced another instance of communicating with fish. In this case it was a single fish, a huge grouper that weighed several hundred pounds. My friend John knew exactly where this giant grouper hung out, about ten miles offshore on the coral reef. And when he'd dive in that vicinity and make certain grunting noises, the big grouper would come to him, cuddle against him, peer into his eyes through his diving mask, and generally follow him around like a giant puppy dog.

John would make his grunting sounds and the grouper would respond with other sounds. "There clearly was something going on here," explained John, "but I never knew just how much it understood. I think it was just the fact that we were communicating . . . I wasn't trying to manipulate its life, and it wasn't trying to manipulate mine."

136

One day the giant grouper appeared no more. John, after asking around, found that a spearfisherman had killed it.

Learning to listen is very important in developing rapport with all wildlife. Most of us hear far more than registers in our consciousness, simply because we shut out sound. In many cases, particularly for those of us who live in noisy urban environments, that is a protective device. Over a period of time, listening to sirens and blaring automobile horns, factory hums, the roar of traffic, and the staccato din of construction tends to dull the sense of hearing. We simply insulate our brain against registering such sounds. In effect, we're diminishing our ability to hear. Many times we're not even aware of how much noise is around us until we enter a natural area where there is virtually none.

Have you ever heard the sound of complete silence? Have you ever listened to your own steady, methodic heartbeat in your ears? Few of us are ever in a situation where we can enjoy such silence. And yet it should be a day-to-day occurrence. So many people cannot tolerate real silence. They go on outings to the beach, the woodlands, or a lake, camp out and swim and hike. But no matter what activity they're involved in, they have to carry some artificial sound along with them. How many times have you seen people walking through a park carrying a blaring radio? Silence. Intolerable. Yet until you've experienced silence, you cannot possibly begin to develop a keener sense of hearing. Surprisingly, as your hearing improves, very likely so will your sense of smell. The environment conducive to improving one sense seems to have a very positive effect upon the other.

British author Jim Phelan, who spent more than a decade in prison, wrote about the change in sensibilities brought on by prison life:

> The tyro in jail has not only to learn a new language and become adept in minor trickeries. He has to develop new senses, become animal-keen in a thousand ways not known to civilization. Long before the end of my second

year I could tell one warden from another, in the dark and at a distance, by his breathing, by his scent, even by the tiny crackings of his joints. Presently I could smell a cigarette in another man's pocket six feet away, hear the lip-still mutter in church even while a trained warder missed every sound. From the way an official clears his throat, a long-term prisoner will know whether that man is likely to report him for smoking half an hour later—a long-sentence convict is not a person; he is an alert, efficient and predatory animal.

We can learn much from the animal world simply by observation. Note that many of the larger wild animals have large ears. As the wolf in *Little Red Riding Hood* said: "All the better to hear you with." The ears, of course, are deep within the skull, but the flaps—such as those of our own ears—are merely shields or cups to catch sounds, deflecting them into the ear cavity. The deer, for instance, has a much higher hearing capacity than we humans do. The human hearing range is above 16 vibrations per second, expressed as 40,000 cycles per second or cps. The cat can hear better in a range well above the level of human hearing. That's one reason a cat will come more quickly when called by a woman than when called by a man; the sound is a higher frequency, closer to the range to which cats are accustomed. A mouse has an even higher range—up to 100,000 cps. When we hear a mouse squeak, we're hearing only the lower notes. Researchers say that a cat cannot detect many of the ultrasonic sounds a mouse makes either, especially the notes of alarm from one mouse to another.

Therefore, the woodlands through which we walk may be alive with a cacophony of sounds that we cannot even hear, simply because they're beyond the levels that can be picked up by our ears. By stopping frequently, however, and cupping our hands on the back side of each ear flap, we may be able to pick up sounds we did not hear before. Certainly it's a good training exercise in improving hearing. And once you begin to listen to the sounds that come your way, you'll start to sharpen

Bobcats have exceptionally keen hearing. Try cupping your hands behind your ears to improve yours.

and improve your hearing sensibilities. You'll be able to tune in to the flow of life in any particular environment, to pick up the distant noises of a woodpecker searching for a morsel in a dead tree, the snort-snort and pawing communication of a whitetail deer over the ridge, the thousands upon thousands of bird calls that permeate the forest, the sound of a rabbit, the chatter of a squirrel, the chirp of a chipmunk.

Another good beginning exercise is to choose a remote woodland, field, or other natural area away from manmade sounds and sit with your back to a tree or rock. Close your eyes and just listen. Sit there for an hour or two without moving, doing absolutely nothing more than listening to the sounds around you. You'll be amazed how much you can turn up the volume in your hearing mechanism.

Fortunately, I live in a quiet place with few human sounds other than those created by my own family. I'm surrounded by several hundred acres of woodland in a hill and ravine landscape. The trees and the lay of the land itself filter out much of the noise that might come my way. My office and the place where I do all my writing is located in a walk-out basement facing a small lake on the downgrade side of a hill. Sounds travel up the hill from the lake, which is surrounded by a forest of cattails. Much goes on around the lake, as well as in the adjoining woodland.

One summer while working on a book, I was separated from the wild environment outside only by screen doors. Although I was typing at the time, my ears picked up a commotion moving up the hill at rapid pace. It ended at my front door. I rushed out just in time to see a spreadhead viper, or hognose, as they're oftentimes called, overtake a scampering toad. It has long been my policy to interfere with the course of nature as little as possible, so I stood by and watched as the snake, totally unaware of my presence because of its involvement, enveloped the toad and swallowed it. The sounds I had heard were the sounds of a snake chasing the toad up the hill through the grass.

Since many people are fearful of snakes, as well as lizards

and other creepy, crawly things, it's most natural for them to train their ears to hear those creatures while on outings. When the incentive is there, we tend to pay greater attention to such sounds and to listen for them, even if subconsciously. Such creatures make few sounds, of course, but the sounds they do make are distinctive.

Once you've begun to listen, to concentrate on sound, you'll begin to enjoy the vast array of sounds in wild places. They can be, in a sense, like music to your ears. Close your eyes and relax. Initially, don't try to identify the separate sounds. Just listen and enjoy them; leave the labels for later. You'll soon learn to distinguish without even trying. The wind will sound differently as it passes through the limbs of each tree. The rattle of a leaf here, the moan of the wind through pine needles there, the gurgling of a tiny brook, the tittering of birds and mice, the creaking and rubbing of one limb against another, the swish of blades of grass, the chirp of a cricket— all of these are part of the delicately orchestrated range of the wilds. Not only should you be hearing more within the human level, but you soon will come to detect a much greater variety, subtlety, and complexity of sound. You'll be able to hear sounds within sounds, the pitch, rhythm, and all the other nuances of the wild places you visit.

Many creatures depend much more on sounds than we do. Male mosquitoes, for instance, it was discovered in a research project, are attracted to the female by the hum of her wings. When she failed to fly and her wings were still, the male mosquitoes passed up the female. If you've noticed the flight of bats during the twilight of evening, you may have been amazed by their maneuverability. But researchers found that after plugging the ears of a bat, the creature flew erratically and often ran into objects. The same occurred when they muzzled its mouth so it could not utter sounds. For the bat emits an ultrasonic sound that bounces off objects in its path and then returns to the ear like radar, thus permitting these little creatures to avoid running into anything.

Many insects operate under principles closely related to

If you train yourself, as I have, you can pick up the heavy scent of a bear.

sound and their interpretations of it. Often this is part of their defense mechanism. We're unable to hear a number of these sounds simply because they're beyond the pitch we can ascertain, but others are not. We may not understand all we hear, yet we should at least be aware of our lack of knowledge. And we should not attempt to interfere, but instead respect the nature of all creatures around us and the complexities by which they operate.

It is not even necessary for us to interpret all the sounds we hear, but we still can enjoy and respect them. We can learn much by remaining passive yet astute observers. The more we observe, the more we listen, the keener our senses will become.

The sounds we hear are amplified up to twenty-two times by the mechanisms within our own ears before they are transmitted to the brain. But there are objects in the wilds which can amplify sounds, too, and help you better to hear and interpret the world about you. Trees, thick brush, rocks, logs, even old tree stumps can act as natural sound catchers. Sometimes you may be able to find natural troughs that catch and modify sound, such as a rock canyon or a sharp ravine. If you find an old log or tree stump, put your head next to it and listen. Surprising how much more you may be able to hear than you did before. Early in my life I learned there were objects about that conducted sound. A railroad track ran near my father's Kentucky farm, and I learned by placing my ear close to the steel rail that I could hear an approaching train long before it was within sight. The rail conducted the sound of the train many miles.

After you've mastered the technique for listening carefully, you can then begin to qualify sounds and categorize them. Identifying and interpreting sounds eventually becomes important in your quest to learn about the out-of-doors. It is, after all, a part of your education. Without it, you cannot possibly grasp the whole picture. When you're ready for that stage, remember that it's much easier, and more meaningful, if you can watch sounds being made. And to watch them being

143

One test of how well you have adapted yourself to the wild is how close birds (such as these nesting brown pelicans) and animals will let you come to their young.

made means again that you may have to stalk the creature making them.

Everything in nature is interrelated. No creature stands alone but is a part of the web of life. The basic laws of physics apply well here: If you learn to look for these laws, you'll come to realize they are part of a continuous process, enacted a million times over every moment of every day. For every action, there is a counteraction. A disturbance in one part of the forest is picked up and echoed into every nook and cranny. The native Americans learned to read these echoes and to interpret the events that initiated them. To the novice, the entire process seems uncanny. But it is not in the least; to become part of the wilds is to know and understand what goes

144

on there. And once that stage is achieved, it is easy to read the echoes.

Nearly as important as listening—and being able to hear—is the sense of smell. Primitive man probably enjoyed a keen sense of smell and used it extensively to lead him to food. In modern society, we have had little need of the olfactory sense, so we've allowed it to become more and more inactive. In the outdoor world it can be most useful, however, and by using certain exercises plus paying greater attention to the odors you encounter, you still can develop this latent talent. Nature offers a veritable treasure trove of odors; you may even smell water. The odors produced by plants, animals, even rocks or other types of minerals, all are part of the aroma of a wild place.

As with any other sense, a prime means of developing your sense of smell is by concentrating upon it. Sit in a quiet place and breathe normally through your nose. Notice what you're smelling. If there are no odors, move to another location and repeat the same exercise. And all the while you're moving, breathe through your nose, trying to detect the scents in the air. Certain animals and plants are more aromatic than others, of course. We've all smelled a skunk, but have you ever smelled a mushroom or other fungus-type growth? Have you ever smelled musty leaves, or tree bark? Do you know how the earth smells when a farmer has just plowed his field in the spring?

Everything in nature has not only a distinctive appearance, but its own distinctive odor as well. The more you become involved with the outdoors, the more aware of odors you'll become. While camping alone in a vast spruce woods near the Yukon River in Alaska one summer, I went for a hike late in the evening. Since it didn't get dark until around 11 P.M., there was still plenty of light, but nothing seemed to be moving. The woods were unusually quiet. As I walked along, I came suddenly upon the heavy, barnyard-like odor of bear. At first, I scanned the woods around me, standing perfectly still.

145

By developing your hearing and sense of smell, you can often discover the presence of an animal, such as this Bighorn desert sheep, before you see it.

Not a single movement. Then I sniffed the air, turning slowly to try to determine the direction from which it was coming. I couldn't. Neither could I determine whether it was black bear or a grizzly, although experts claim there's a slight difference. I looked for tracks in the soft moss of the forest floor; there were none. I moved slowly on in the direction I initially was headed, making sure I could see well ahead. Above all, I didn't want to surprise a grizzly. Finally, with the waning light heralding darkness, I retraced my steps toward camp. The odor ceased a few hundred yards from camp, but twice during the night I awakened to detect the same scent close by. Never once did I see the bear, but I knew it was in the neighborhood.

A good way to familiarize yourself with the smell of certain animals, whenever you find a den in the woods, or signs that an animal has been through, is to kneel down and sniff the ground. See if you can detect discernible odors that will help you to remember this animal whenever you encounter it again.

Don't limit yourself to the smells of animals. Learn the smells of plants as well. We all know the scent of pine needles; many builders of homes incorporated cedar or pine lining in closets to give clothes an unmistakable fresh fragrance. At almost any time of year certain plants are in bloom, even during winter. Many of those blossoms give off a fragrance. Some of them attract the creatures of the wilds, whether because they like the scent, or because they like to feed upon that particular plant. In those instances, you should take special note. Any scent that attracts animals may work for you as well. Smash some of the blossoms, or leaves, and rub them into your clothing, on your skin, and on your shoes.

While odors in the wilds are something that can enrich your own outdoor experience, you must also remember that you, too, give off a distinctive odor that can tip off creatures to your presence, thus alarming them perhaps before you even see them. Early hunters used to bury their clothes in an earthen mound a few days before they dressed in them for the hunt. You may not want to do that, but you can rub them

147

down with pine needles, or other plants or odors familiar to an area. In some cases, I've used skunk cabbage, which has a very pungent odor; other times, in areas where there is wild catnip, I've used that; and sometimes Queen Anne's lace, or wild carrot. Be careful not to use anything that isn't found in the area you're visiting. If the scent is foreign, animals will pick it up instantly and move away. A strange scent to them is almost like waving a red flag.

A good way to sensitize yourself for smelling plants is to close your eyes, turn around two or three times, and then lie down among them. Still keeping your eyes closed, try to identify the plants around you. Then open your eyes and see just where the plants are located and how many you have correctly identified. Do not pull up plants, but you may break a steam or leaf from one and try to identify it by smell.

Last, remember you also have a sense of touch. While it's unlikely you'll ever be sufficiently skillful to stalk up close enough to most animals to touch them, there are many other creatures that actually will come to you. Try to eliminate your prejudices and allow them to crawl on you. Note the sensation made by a caterpillar, for instance, as it crawls upon your skin. Using some morsels of food, try to attract birds to light and feed out of your hand, and note the sensation you feel as they peck at the palm. Lie down and allow whatever comes your way to crawl over you, exploring in its own way. Can you do it? It is all a part of learning the art of touch. For learning to touch is also learning to be touched.

Next, move about a natural area touching almost everything you see—except toxic plants, of course, or things to which you may be allergic. When you see a tree, move close and touch the bark, not just with your hands but with your body. Hug the tree. Put your face against the trunk and allow yourself to think about the sensation. What does the bark feel like against your skin? Do the same with flowers and plants. Find a dead log in the forest and touch it in the same way. How does it differ from a live tree? All these things can be a part of your education, of learning to distinguish the difference between the texture of one thing and another.

Birds and animals are seldom unaware of your presence but like this Louisiana heron, they will often tolerate you if they feel no threat is involved.

Listening, smelling, touching—each of these is part of the process of adapting yourself to the wilds. To know nature is to develop a oneness with it. To be a good observer of wildlife, to gain an understanding of the plant and animal world, is to know it as well as though it were a part of your own self.

Chapter 9

That Amazing Sixth Sense

Do animals possess a sixth sense? The question is asked many times; seldom are there substantial answers. Many researchers place this unexplained phenomenon under the category of instinct. But some humans, and perhaps all of us, have a certain amount of it.

Anthropologists claim that ancient man possessed a much higher degree of instinct than we do today simply because he exercised it so much more. As our keenness of hearing and scent has diminished during past generations, so has our sense of instinct. Yet wild animals still use instinct on a constant and continuing basis.

Every time I think about extrasensory perception (ESP), or instinct, if you will, I'm reminded of the story of a farmer who years ago found a tiny baby bluejay in his yard. It had fallen from the nest, and rather than risk having it caught by the family cat, he took the baby bird home. Together, the farmer and his wife raised it. The jay became virtually a member of the family. Because it was always getting into something it should not, they named the bird Pesty. It was most appropriate. Pesty would lift the blossoms from a bouquet and take a bath in the water. Any time soup was served at meals, everyone had better watch his bowl—Pesty considered it prime bathwater. He also immensely enjoyed picking out the goodies from the soup bowl.

One day the farmer brought Pesty some nice fat fishing worms from a field he was plowing, and the bird so much enjoyed this newfound delicacy that he became a special buddy of the farmer from that day on. Whenever the farmer sat in his easy chair during the evenings reading the paper, Pesty perched on his shoulder. And when he went to bed at night, the farmer always allowed a little time for cuddling and paying special attention to Pesty.

The bluejay had shown no signs of possessing a sixth sense, however, and the farmer and his wife did not feel there was any special communication taking place between themselves and the bluejay. It had become fully domesticated, never accepted by the wild birds that gathered in the farmer's yard. In fact, they would fight whenever Pesty was outside. But one day when no other birds were around, Pesty escaped through an open door. The farmer and his wife had to leave for town an hour later, but they could not find their pet. As it was a beautiful spring day, they decided to leave Pesty outside until they returned . . . Pesty was never seen again. They searched the entire area the following day and for days afterward, but the bird had vanished.

Summer turned to fall, fall to winter. Then finally spring and early summer returned. The farmer's wife was in the kitchen when she heard the wild birds outside making a great commotion. Rushing out, she saw perched on the garage roof a beautiful bluejay. It was not Pesty, but it looked similar. It obviously was a very young bird, yet it didn't act wild. When she offered it a cookie, it came to light on her hand and nibble at the cookie. When she went to sit on the patio, the bird followed. And when she went inside, the bird followed her

Does this great white heron possess a sixth sense that allows it to know I will not harm it?

153

there, too, flying directly to the perch over the kitchen sink that Pesty had used a year before.

The farmer came in from the fields that night, sat down to dinner, and the bluejay flew to perch on his shoulder just as Pesty had done. It had been nearly a year since Pesty had gone, and this bluejay was so young it could not even have been hatched at the time of Pesty's disappearance. Yet it acted just as Pesty had acted, roosted where Pesty roosted, and sat on the farmer's shoulder in exactly the same way its predecessor had done. Whether this was instinct or whether some uncanny communication had taken place, one will never know.

One of the strangest stories I came across took place at the Great Swamp National Wildlife Refuge, just twenty minutes from Times Square, in New Jersey. An official told me that a few months earlier they had opened a portion of the refuge for a controlled deer hunt. "The whitetail population had gotten out of hand," he explained. "It had been several years since we'd allowed hunting." Many of the people living in the urban areas around the swamp opposed any thought of hunting the whitetail, however, and the matter became quite controversial. The plans continued, but the refuge management agreed to keep portions of the area closed to hunters.

"A funny thing happened," the official said, "and I would not have believed it had I not seen it happen. For a couple of days prior to the hunt, we spotted numerous deer leaving the area to be hunted, swimming the Passaic River into the area that was closed to hunting. It was as though someone had tipped them off. And hunting season hadn't even begun."

Many unusual animal stories have been passed down through the years. While working closely with wild animals in my profession as a nature photojournalist, I've transmitted unspoken thoughts to them without gestures and had them respond almost as though they could fully understand my wishes. A few times, I've felt that had to be nothing more than coincidence. But as the occurrences multiplied, I began to feel that indeed some type of mental telepathy was at work.

Once I'd been working with four grizzlies in Montana, at-

When I photographed Kodiak bears on Kodiak Island, Alaska, a guide advised me that bears could sense a gun—even if it was concealed.

tempting to capture photographs for a magazine article I'd been assigned to do. To get a larger concentration of grizzlies than the single bear one usually sees in the wild, I had gone to a small garbage dump in a national forest. I arrived early one afternoon and staked out my location. Soon, four huge grizzlies approached single file across a meadow near the dump. As they came closer and closer, now and then breaking into a short jog, I took my first pictures. The bears showed absolutely no interest in me, other than to look my way and sniff the air a couple of times. They were intent on feeding at the dump. Once there, they gobbled up just about everything edible they could get their paws on.

Moving closer but always being careful to keep open an avenue of escape, I began to concentrate on their activities. A half hour passed, then an hour. Occasionally one of them would look my way, sometimes stand up on his hind feet for a better view, then resume eating. I decided I was never going to get any good pictures of bears at the garbage dump. Capturing the kinds of shots I wanted, with the bears facing the camera—and not just one, but several of them—simply wasn't going to happen.

It was then I decided to try some psychology on the bears. They had already eaten a good deal, and if mental telepathy would work at all, it certainly had a better chance with animals that were no longer famished.

No words were spoken, but I concentrated on positive thoughts filled with compliments and respect for these great silver-tipped bears. When they were turned away from me, I asked them to turn around, facing the camera. At first, absolutely nothing happened. And then, as the August afternoon wore on, I began to get responses. When I asked, the bears did turn my way. And sometimes one or two of them would stand up, staring in my direction. Since I was using a 500 mm telephoto lens on my Hasselblad camera, I was able virtually to fill the frame without getting any closer. I fully respected the bears and would never approach closer than seventy-five to one hundred feet during the time they were feeding. As a backup, I'd located several trees nearby that would provide me with an easy escape route should any of them charge me.

No charge nor any other threat came, however. All afternoon, the bears and I worked at the garbage dump, and as the light began to fade in the evening, I left them there and returned to my camp five miles away in another part of the forest. It was almost as though I had come to know them; I wondered if they had indeed experienced some of the same feelings.

The bear episode is only one instance. I have had—and continue to have—a multitude of such experiences. The results are not always the same, or even similar, but many times I've walked away from encounters with specific wild animals awed by the unspoken communication that occurred. And my belief in extrasensory communication with wildlife is shared by a number of other people who have worked closely with animals.

A few years ago when I was on Kodiak Island in Alaska photographing huge Kodiak bear for *The Island,* I chanced to meet, on separate occasions, two old-time big game guides. Between them the two had more than eighty years' experience at plying their trade.

"If you want to get close to the big bears," one of them told me, "don't take a gun with you." I expressed surprise, since the Alaska Fish & Game Commission had recommended that I carry a gun of at least 30-06 or larger caliber with me at all times for protection in the backcountry.

"If the bear you come across has had experience with hunters," the guide explained, "perhaps has been shot at or wounded at some time in the past, it'll either charge you or run away. Either way, you're not likely to get good pictures. If you don't carry a gun, you'll have a lot more success," he added.

"Even if the gun is concealed?" I asked.

"Even if the gun is concealed," he answered.

The second guide told me essentially the same thing. Nei-

157

ther man believes in ESP, but both said the bears, as do all wild animals, possess what they called certain instincts.

Some scientists who have closely studied the interrelationships between man and wildlife claim ESP does not exist. One, Dr. Thomas Sebeok, director of the Research Center for Animal Communication at Indiana University, and an internationally renowned authority on the subject, says simply: "There is no such thing as extrasensory perception. Not in animals, not in man. What we read as ESP," he goes on, "is actually a high sensitivity development to other senses, perhaps a combination of those senses. Animals that respond to our thoughts are not responding to anything beyond simple reality. They're reading certain visible signs—our manner, our expressions, our appearance, our gestures. That's all."

Many nonscientists who work in the field with all kinds of animals, including marine life, feel differently. And so do some scientists.

Two psychologists in southern Florida who have worked with dolphins in an experimental program for autistic and retarded children say there are definite, distinctive interreactions between the dolphins and the children. One of them told me: "The reaction of the dolphins to retarded children is much different than it is with normal people. And we've had retarded children, on the other hand, who acted close to normal when they were with a dolphin. One five-year-old boy who was believed incapable of uttering a word because he had never made any attempt to talk suddenly spoke words to the dolphins."

What perception takes place between the dolphins and retarded children perhaps will never be known, but observers who work closely with both say the relationship is very special. Is it ESP, or something else?

During the 1950s when I was a high school student, I used to amaze my friends by using what they called ESP. They would try to sneak up behind me, and invariably I would turn to face them when they were only a couple of footsteps away. It wasn't that I could hear them, but I could feel their presence on the back of my neck. It was as though I

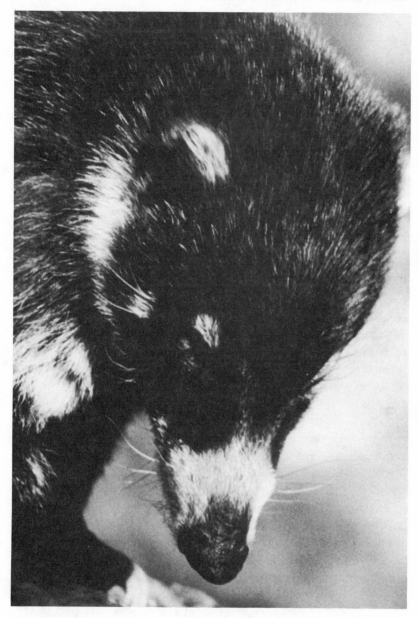

The coatimundi of the Southwest, a member of the raccoon family, which many people credit with great intelligence.

159

could sense their body heat. ESP? No, I think not. I believe instead it was merely my own heightened sensitivity that told me they were close behind. Snakes use a similar means of perception, especially the pit vipers that can detect minute changes in temperature.

The numerous incredible stories involving animals and their remarkable instincts have led to many deeply involved studies over the years. Rather than ESP, these studies have assumed the designation *anpsi*, using "Psi-," the twenty-third letter of the Greek alphabet, preceded by "an-," indicating animal. Anpsi refers to an extraordinary or unexplained communication between animal and man, an animal and its environment, or between two animals.

The uncanny homing ability of animals has been demonstrated and documented many times. National Park Service rangers in Yellowstone National Park have on numerous occasions captured bears, both blacks and grizzlies, that have caused problems by molesting tourists along the roadside or in the campgrounds. The bears have been marked with a splotch of paint and transported as much as one hundred miles away to be dropped in a totally different area. Some of these bears have returned almost as quickly as the rangers to their home territory.

As a small lad, I was amazed at the number of cats that continuously turned up at my father's farm. They liked it there because we had dairy cows and there was always lots of warm fresh milk to drink. But my father was unhappy with all the cats and many times would sack up the strays in burlap bags, then transport them thirty miles away to the other side of the county. Often the cats returned to our farm, usually taking no more than three or four days to make the journey.

For a long time, it was felt that fish used some sort of mental telepathy, or anpsi, to guide their return to their natal streams. This was thought to be especially true of salmon, which spawn in streams, often near the headwaters and in the tributaries of great rivers, are flushed out to sea where they roam for several years, and then return to exactly the same place to spawn. More recently researchers have found that the

160

A psychological trick enabled me to get several grizzlies in one shot.

fish actually identify the waters of the place where they were born by smell. To prove this point, Dr. A. D. Hasler caught three hundred salmon returning in two arms of the Issaquah River in Washington and blocked the nostrils of half the fish. The ones free to breathe and smell returned normally to their natal locations; the ones with blocked nostrils blundered about, unable to go in any one direction.

Many stories have been told—and factually supported— about animals that have traveled long distances, following an uncanny homing instinct after being separated from their families. One such journey concerned Bobbie, a collie-mix who was lost from his family while the family was visiting relatives in Indiana back in 1923. The family looked desperately for the dog for several days but finally gave up and motored back to their Oregon home in August. Bobbie, taking a route totally different from that of his owners, showed up at home the following February, after traveling some three thousand miles across all kinds of terrain in all kinds of weather. His journey was retraced by an investigating team from the Oregon Humane Society, which interviewed dozens of people Bobbie had befriended along the way. So remarkable was his return that the dog was presented with the keys to the city and became one of history's most honored canine heroes.

The late Dr. J. B. Rhine of Duke University collected more than five hundred case histories of animals who possessed and displayed some special instinct. Among them were a number of examples involving homing instincts, normally associated with pigeons. His subjects, however, were dogs, cats, and even horses. One anpsi case that merited Dr. Rhine's investigation was a cat named Sugar, owned by Stacy Woods, once a school principal in Anderson, California. The Woods family moved to a farm in Oklahoma, but decided, since the cat was dreadfully frightened of traveling in the car, to leave Sugar with some neighbors. Two thousand miles later, Sugar showed up at the farm and leaped up on Mr. Woods's shoulder.

Such remarkable stories are not new but have been told for centuries. One concerns a famous talking horse belonging to John Bank in sixteenth-century France. The horse, it is claimed, could, by stamping with its hoof, indicate the totals of a pair of dice totally concealed from its view. More recently, in a red barn near Richmond, Virginia, a horse named Lady performed unbelievable feats for nearly thirty years, even predicting correctly the outcome of the presidential election between Harry Truman and Thomas Dewey. Dr. Rhine camped outside the barn for weeks, studying the methods used by Lady without reaching any conclusive results. But he said the horse unquestionably possessed some sort of psychic power.

Some people believe such acts to be the results of love and affection, or of a special closeness to a master. Dr. Karlis Osis of the Parapsychology Laboratory at Duke University showed that special homing instincts displayed by certain animals might indeed be the result of considerable influence through affectional bonds. But this is not always the case. Most parapsychology researchers believe some sort of psychic power plays a role in these extraordinary abilities. Bill Schul, author of *The Psychic Power of Animals*, recalled a time when his horse stopped and refused to budge just before a bolt of lightning struck a spot on the trail ahead of him. The night Abraham Lincoln was assassinated, his dog began howling and racing erratically around the White House a full hour before the President was shot.

Dr. Hans Bender of the Freiburg Institute of Parapsychology in Germany reports the case of a duck that created an uproar in Freiburg Park just before the worst Allied bombing raid that country had experienced in the final days of World War II. The duck repeated its alarm every fifteen minutes until the bombs began to fall, sending hundreds of people to safety in air-raid shelters. The duck itself died in the bombing.

The ties between man and animal were further confirmed by the experiments of Dr. Aristide Esser at Rockland State Hospital in New York. In one experiment, he placed a boxer in a soundproof room some distance from the dog's mistress, who was put into another soundproof room. The doctor then had a stranger enter the mistress's room and make threats, flinging her about. The dog, which was attached to an electrocardiogram, also became excited at that very same moment, its heartbeat shooting up violently.

Mental telepathy? Who knows what strange things occur between minds? One of the oddest experiences ever recorded was back in 1922, when Lord Carnarvon sponsored the English expedition that discovered the accursed tomb of ancient Egyptian ruler Tutankhamen, King Tut. Four months later, Lord Carnarvon dropped dead in Cairo. At precisely that moment, all the lights in the city went out. Also precisely at that moment, at the nobleman's estate some two thousand miles away in England, his favorite dog uttered a strange cry and then fell dead.

The ability of animals to feel the presence of danger is phenomenal. The Chinese people began relying on animals to predict earthquakes about ten years ago. In February of 1975, alarmed by a peak of frenzy in the animal world, Chinese officials evacuated a million residents from the city of Haicheng just before an earthquake reduced it to rubble.

In the United States, when the terrible earthquake of

163

Gaddy's Wild Goose Refuge, Ansonville, North Carolina
(Photo by Jim Page, Department of Conservation & Development, North Carolina)

164

1959 struck the area just beyond West Yellowstone, Montana, residents of the area reported strange behavior among animals. Guy Hanson of the U.S. Forest Service, who lived on the outskirts of town, recalls that night very well: "It was a beautiful moonlit night, and I had a pack of hounds. The dogs first started barking about 9 P.M., later howling something outrageous about 11 P.M., and I got up to quiet them down. The first tremor had not yet been felt, but the dogs must have sensed it. They quieted down temporarily, though, and I had just started back into the house when it hit."

The power of the quake hurled Hanson to the ground, even though the epicenter was about eighteen miles away.

"We have tall trees in our yard, and they began to shake, their tops swaying back and forth, then whipping through the air. The windows in the house were rattling, and when I tried to open the door, it was jammed. The dogs kept right on barking and barking. It is clear to me now they knew something terrible was about to happen at least two hours before it happened."

Numerous theories have been offered to explain why animals can forecast such disturbances. In the case of earthquakes, some scientists believe that the animals, because of their highly developed sensitivity, can actually feel the tiny movements in the earth days before an earthquake occurs. Others say gaseous odors released deep within the ground escape to the surface hours, sometimes days, prior to a quake, thus alerting the animals that something is wrong. They react accordingly.

While many of these changes within the earth are beyond the perception of man, they are not beyond those of animals. For example, consider how minute magnetic field changes affect the homing pigeon. On an average, the earth's geomagnetic fields reach 60,000 gammas at the poles and 30,000 gammas at the equator, a gamma being a basic measure of magnetism. Cornell University biologists Timy Larkin and the late William Keeton found during their research that homing pigeons, like super-sensitive magnetic compasses, can be thrown off their course by magnetic field changes of as little as

30 gammas. Such minute magnetic fluctuations also affect the flights of termites, honeybees, beetles, sea gulls, and other creatures. Prior to earthquakes or magnetic field disturbances, whole flocks of wild Canada geese have actually flown into obstacles. Since magnetic changes of 10 to 30 gammas have been recorded preceding earthquakes in Turkey, Japan, and China, it's understandable why some animals act irrationally hours before the quake occurs.

When one thinks of the super-sensitivity of animals and remembers that all of nature is exploding with ultrasounds and infrasounds that are easily detected by many creatures, it's not hard to understand why they could become disoriented by the bombardment of high-frequency screeches made by microfracturing rocks deep within the earth prior to a major quake.

In some cases when animals react to human responses, researchers claim this could be partially explained by a sensitivity to the pheromones released by each person. Research on these chemical reactions to different emotional responses continues. But many other totally unexplained phenomena remain, which are difficult to attribute to anything except a type of mental telepathy that comes from the oneness that unites all life.

The geese at Gaddy's Wild Goose Refuge are said to have reacted to Mr. Gaddy's death. (Photo by Jim Page, Department of Conservation & Development, North Carolina)

167

Chapter 10

Wisdom of the Weeds

Do plants actually possess thoughts? Can they talk? Are they able to respond and react to humans, as well as other creatures? Is there wisdom in a weed? These questions have resulted in considerable speculation and research since 1960. Even before that time, such highly acclaimed plant sociologists as Dr. George Washington Carver and Luther Burbank created stirring controversies, some of which resulted in respectable beliefs about the world of plants. And rightly so.

Mankind is more dependent upon the plant world than the animal world. Some 25 million square miles of green plants virtually cover the surface of the planet. Without them, we could neither breathe nor eat. From spring until fall, on the under side of every leaf are a million movable lips, all devouring carbon dioxide and creating that incredible element, oxygen, so necessary for the life of every breathing creature on earth.

People who are interested in communicating with the

Using a camera—even a very simple one—will help document your animal experiences.

world about them should not look only at animals; they should also pay increasingly intensive attention to plants. I like to think of plants as the intermediaries of life, providing a vital link between humans and animals. The greater percentage of animals are herbivores, and of the 380 billion tons of food consumed by humanity each year, the higher percentage comes from plants. Though plants play such an important role in our society, many people tend either to ignore their existence or to take them for granted.

Except in controlled laboratory research projects, there's no evidence of plants initiating any communication with most creatures of the mammal world. But there is a mountain of evidence that grows daily of plants' receptivity and responses not only to humans and animals, but to the insect world and to each other. Just how it's done remains a mystery; there are

169

several theories. The most acceptable one states that communication occurs by means of chemicals, but there's also considerable belief that plants possess extrasensory perception, or ESP.

Insofar as is known, plants lack a central nervous system or brain power. They cannot think. But in some cases, their responses to external stimuli might tend to make one believe they can. Even in ancient Greece, Aristotle held that plants have souls but no sensation, a dogma that survived until the eighteenth century, when the man often known as the grandfather of modern botany—Carl von Linné—declared that plants only differ from animals in that they cannot move. Charles Darwin shot down this theory, however, when he proved that every tendril of a plant has the ability to move independently. Early in this century, Raoul France, a Viennese botanist, gave more credence to Darwin's experiments when he said that plants move their bodies as freely, easily, and gracefully as the most skilled animal or human. The only reason we don't appreciate the fact, he said, is because the plants do so at a much slower pace.

"No plant," said France, "is without movement. All growth is a series of movements. Plants are constantly preoccupied with bending, turning and quivering."

Take a vine, for instance. The tendril of a vine sweeps a full circle every sixty-seven minutes, according to France's research. When it finds a perch, it starts to curve around the object within twenty seconds, and within an hour has wound itself so firmly it is hard to tear away. The tendril then curls itself like a corkscrew and in so doing raises the vine to itself. The next tendril on the vine repeats the process.

Plants develop many protective devices. Some create thorns on their surface, others a bitter taste, some a gummy secretion that either kills or repels insects or other threats. Certain plants—the carnivores such as the pitcher plant, sundew, bladderwort, or Venus's-flytrap—actually entrap insects and other creatures and devour them. Yet they will not react to inanimate objects such as stones, metal, or wooden sticks.

Some plants contain such remarkable metaphysical quali-

If you've never used a camera before, practice before loading it with film.

ties that they can predict catastrophes. The Indian licorice plant, for instance, is keenly sensitive to all types of magnetic or electrical impulses. Botanists in Kew Gardens in London found the licorice plant reliable in predicting such phenomena as tornadoes, earthquakes, volcanic eruptions, and even hurricanes.

Whether plants possess ESP or SSP (super-sensitive perception, as some scientists prefer to term it) is still a matter of speculation, but some very convincing research has been done lending credibility to the belief that plants do indeed feel and react with either positive or negative responses to certain external stimuli.

171

One of the foremost contemporary researchers in this field, credited in recent times with opening the Pandora's box to science, is Cleve Backster, who operated a polygraph (lie detector) school in New York City. In 1966, on a lackadaisical day, he began experimenting with his office plants, attaching electrodes to the leaves to see if the polygraph machine would pick up any responses. The results were nothing short of remarkable. And from that point on, Backster, subsidized by grants from all sorts of foundations, began more sophisticated tests which would lead to some amazing results.

Among the tests he ultimately ran was one of intended harm to a dracaena plant. The machine recorded no unusual response when Backster dipped the leaves of the plant into a cup of hot coffee he was drinking, but when he decided moments later to burn the leaves with a match, the plant responded dramatically on the machine even before he went to get the matches. Just the thought of burning the leaves without any outward action on Backster's part had caused the plant to react.

Later, Backster devised a scheme to determine if plants possessed the ability to remember. Using six of his polygraph students, most of whom were policemen, Backster first blindfolded them. Next, he had them draw names from a hat. On one of the slips of paper were instructions for that person to violently extract a plant from its pot, throw it on the floor, and stomp it. Another sister plant would be located nearby in the same room, but would be untouched by students. Neither Blackster nor any other student was to know the identity of the student selected to do the dirty work, hence the reason for the blindfolds.

Backster attached the polygraph machine to the second plant, which witnessed the atrocity. Then he had each of the six students go into the room, one by one. The plant indicated no reaction whatsoever to the first five students, but when the sixth student went in, who had been the one to harm the other plant so violently, the polygraph needle went wild.

In another SSP experiment, Backster used synchronized stopwatches to record precise moments when there was reac-

I recommend two lenses to my beginning students—a wide-angle and a short-length telephoto.

tion from his plants. He left the office with his plants hooked up to the machine and drove over into New Jersey some fifteen miles away. He was careful not to think of returning to New York until he had reached his prearranged destination. Then, when he decided to turn around, he noted the time on the stopwatch he was carrying and recorded it. Back in the office, he noted unusual responses from his plants which coincided precisely with the time he decided to return.

The fact that plants have instant responses was again demonstrated late one night in Backster's New York office by a philodendron. Two authors, Sheila Ostrander and Lynn Schroeder—who in 1974 published the *Handbook of PSI Discoveries*—and a NASA engineer were visiting Backster at his office. No experiment was under way, but the philo-

173

dendron was still hooked up to a recording device. Ostrander and Schroeder reported that the conversation rambled, and finally got around to the rising cost of rents in New York City. The recording device showed absolutely no response from the plant all that time until someone jokingly remarked to Backster that if the costs of rents kept going up, he might not have enough money left to feed the plants. The needle of the recorder immediately shot up and everyone laughed—except the philodendron.

Cleve Backster, who later established the Backster Research Foundation in New York, believes plants can receive and respond to instant communication, even if the sender is thousands of miles away. "It is possible," he once said, "that some process about which we have not yet learned provides such instant communication through electromagnetic forces." Backster does not use the term "telepathy," but perhaps that is the psychic force with which the plants are dealing. And if it works with plants, it's certainly conceivable it might also be found in animals, particularly in creatures of the wild that have not been associated directly with man.

Uncanny, unbelievable? Not if you know and believe in plants. It's the same relationship that exists between people who supposedly have "green thumbs" and their plants. The plants respond because people with green thumbs have an affinity for their charges, talk to them as though they were equals or certainly living beings, shower them with love, and often even play music for them. And the plants apparently respond.

A couple of experiments with music were enough to set the scientific world on its ear, especially nonbelievers in plant SSP. In the late 1950s, Eugene Canby of Wainfleet, Ontario, in Canada, a farmer and engineer, broadcast violin sonatas by Bach to test-plots of wheat. Even though the soil where the test-plots were located was inferior to other nearby soils where wheat was growing, the test-plot listening to Bach produced 66 percent greater yields than did the other plots. And the grains were larger and heavier as well.

Shortly thereafter, at Normal, Illinois, botanist and agri-

When photographing in woodland, I prefer foggy or light rainy days.

cultural researcher George Smith planted corn and soybeans in test-plots in identical greenhouses. Everything was well controlled—temperature and humidity, soil conditions, amounts of fertilizer, and supervision. In one greenhouse, he installed a small record player and for twenty-four hours a day played Gershwin's *Rhapsody in Blue*. The Gershwin seedlings sprouted almost two weeks earlier than the others, and their stems were much healthier. Smith was amazed, but he remained skeptical.

In 1961, he continuously broadcast classical and semi-classical music to a small plot of Embro 44XE hybrid corn from the time it was planted to the day of harvest. The plot

175

produced twenty more bushels than a test-plot of similar size which heard no music. Smith also noted that the musically grown corn grew more rapidly, was more uniform in size, and matured earlier.

Having grown up on a farm myself, I knew three relatives who definitely possessed green thumbs. Two were older cousins who farmed separately within two or three miles of my parent's farm in western Kentucky. One of them had the reputation of being able to grow anything, anywhere, even on a rock. It was almost as though his plants were part of him. Garden vegetables responded to him even when they received little cultivation. They just grew. But he spent a lot of time with them, and he always said that along with the seed he sowed, he broadcast positive thoughts.

My mother, to this day, has a special way with plants. She'll have garden plants already growing before winter is over. Tomatoes will be producing in her garden a good two weeks to a month before those of her neighbors. Her garden looks lush and well kept, the plants producing heavily even in bad, drought-ridden years. My mother says it's because she cares for the plants and gives them such TLC (tender loving care). "TLC," she adds, "is worth much more than commercial fertilizer to plants. They flourish on it."

A Milwaukee florist who pipes music into his greenhouse observed what he called "striking differences" in the flowers and plants. "My plants germinate quicker, bloom more abundantly, and the blooms last longer. They're brighter, prettier, and more striking to the eye," he added.

What is it about music that plants respond to? Scientists believe it to be the vibrations created. Plants don't necessarily respond favorably to all music, though. Dorothy Retallack, working in Colorado on her college degree, experimented with all kinds of music for special credits. Retallack found that more than 50 percent of her plants, when exposed to jazz recordings of Duke Ellington's *Soul Call* and some renditions by Louis Armstrong, leaned as much as 20 degrees toward the loudspeakers. Growth, she said, was considerably more abundant than in a comparable silent chamber nearby. Her experi-

176

The author equipped for a day of photographing in Alaska.

ments caught the eye of the press, especially when she found that some plants withered and died when exposed to hard rock while others flourished when listening to classical or semi-classical music. Her findings were later recorded on time-lapse cameras by CBS, and she and her plants were a featured attraction on a Walter Cronkite newscast in 1970.

The role of music in bridging the communication gap is not limited to plants. Wild animals also have responded favorably to the sounds of music. Author Robert Franklin Leslie told me he used to play the harmonica to bears around his wilderness campfire at night, and they would sit on their haunches and sway in unison to the music. Wolves and coyotes reportedly will do the same, sometimes joining in with a chorus of their own. I've never heard of an angry bear being stopped by the sound of music, but if I were being charged by a great grizzly and had the opportunity, I'd certainly play a wild harmonica. And unless a substantial tree were nearby to provide a quick escape route, the harp might just be the margin between life and death.

While plants cannot move away from impending danger, they have developed a tremendous system of protection. Some plants contain as many as eight toxins; others can change their poison from one year to the next. And recent findings indicate that some arboreal species can communicate silently through the air at distances of up to seventy-five to one hundred feet. University of Washington biologist David Rhoades found that healthy trees up to seventy-five feet away from those that had been attacked by either disease or insects would start secreting poisonous chemicals designed to protect them against the onslaught.

At first, Rhoades felt some sort of signal was being transmitted through the root system; he dug up several trees to look for those root connections, but found none. Across the country at Dartmouth, entomologist Jack Schultz began experimenting with several individually potted sugar maples and poplars housed within a Plexiglass chamber. When he damaged the leaves of one tree, undamaged ones under the same dome also began to grow less nutritional leaves. Yet a control

Wildlife photographers can benefit from using camouflage clothing such as hunters wear.

179

group of trees in a separate nearby dome, with a separate air supply, failed to react at all. Both Rhoades and Schultz believe plants to be akin to animals. Said Schultz: "Plants are just very slow animals; the only thing they can't do is run away."

Patricia Moorten of Moorten's Desertland Botanical Garden at Palm Springs, California, finds plants as filled with character as she does human beings. She and her late husband spent years studying and collecting plants from all the great deserts of the world. Much of their work, however, was restricted specifically to the deserts of the southwestern United States and Baja in Mexico. "Plants respond to emotions just as humans do," she said. "You treat them nicely, and they respond positively. Treat them badly, and they will wither and die."

Botanist Marie Desbiez at the University of Clermont in France has carried out experiments which she says illustrate conclusively that plants, although without nervous systems, do have the ability to store and transmit information. "And apparently," she says, "some plants have the ability to sense objects in their paths."

Marcel Vogel, a researcher on plant parapsychology in California, ran a series of tests in 1971 to determine plant response to affectionate thoughts. Attaching a galvanometer for measuring the plant's responses to a philodendron, he stood before the plant, completely relaxed, and showered it with affectionate thoughts. Each time he did this, a series of positive oscillations were recorded on the chart. Vogel also experienced the sensation of feeling an outpouring of energy and affection from the plant on the palms of his outstretched hands, which were not even touching the leaves. After about five minutes, no further reactions were recorded. Vogel concluded he had tapped all the energy from the plant and now would have to wait until some of it had been restored before continuing the test.

Luther Burbank, who became known as the guru of both orchard and garden in the United States, claimed he talked to his charges. He once confided that when experimenting with

My son Billy, at age fifteen, building rapport with a prairie dog in South Dakota.

cactus plants, he tried to talk them out of their thorns. "You have nothing to fear," he would say to them. "You don't need your defensive thorns. I will protect you." And eventually this most useful plant of the desert emerged in a thornless variety.

While researchers have, beyond question, recorded responses from plants with highly sophisticated equipment, there's little chance you'll be able to feel any return from plants you communicate with in the wilds. But it's good to keep in mind that plants do understand, respond, and record what goes on around them. If they by some chance possess the awesome ability to communicate with the animal world and are actually doing so, then why shouldn't we utilize these talents and nurture our own desire to grow closer to all creatures of the natural world?

Many philosophers believe that the same oneness that applies to all life in the animal world also extends to the plant and insect world. Developing that feeling of oneness, and understanding your relationship to all other forms of life, is most important. Generating such philosophical concepts can only be an asset in attaining greater rapport with every type of creature in order to bring about a greater understanding of life itself.

Don't limit yourself to taking pictures of wildlife—take photographs of plants, scenery, signs, and any related activities.

183

Chapter 11

Capturing Images

$c\!A$n excellent means of recording your "oneness-of-life" with the world of nature is the camera. Regardless of what type of equipment you own, you may utilize it to capture on film reminders that grow more valuable with the years. Memories are great, but they're so much better when implemented by the pictures you've collected.

How many times have you heard someone exclaim over a view before them, or an encounter with certain types of wildlife: "If only I could get a picture of that!" There's absolutely no reason why anyone can't get a picture of almost anything the eye sees. It just takes a little more effort and enough desire to act.

If you need an excuse for wandering in the woods or a wild place, what better reason could there be than capturing images of what you see? Whether it is just for a few hours' interlude in the park or a lengthy photographic examination of the wilderness, the urge is there (perhaps an ancient one) to communicate with the pantheon of nature through depiction.

Nature photography provides an instant bond between

oneself and the subject, for the act of making an image is a very introspective and personal one. For the moment, all else is forgotten. It is an adventure steeped in exhilaration. A slice of life may be forever documented along with your own confrontation of self.

Once when I talked with Ansel Adams, the venerable godfather of photography, I asked him as he looked back over his eighty-odd years what his most cherished experiences were. Right away, he replied they were the instances when he had been able to capture the essence of a particular moment on film. "When you have captured it well," he said, "you know you've touched upon the spirit of life."

Capturing the essence of a particular moment is not always an easy task, but if you carry a camera with you as you venture closer to the natural world, you'll soon find yourself recording a good deal more than you may have thought possible. Not everyone is destined to be a great nature photographer, but you can add tremendous spice to your outdoor experience by carrying along a camera.

If you've ever been a hunter, you'll find the camera can be more fun, easier to carry, and far more rewarding than a gun. You may still use many of the same techniques—the same stalking methods, the same awareness—and rise to the same challenges. You can't eat the results, but you can certainly capture some conversation pieces of which you will be proud in years to come.

Anyone can take pictures. With today's versatile, lightweight, and simplified equipment, plus some very fine brands of film, you can learn many of the basics about good photography within a matter of minutes. From that point on, it's a question of applying many of the techniques we've discussed in other chapters, techniques which will help you get close to animals, understanding them to the point where you'll be able to predict their moves before they make them. Patience, timing, and technique are important assets, but those qualities are just as important for developing a more meaningful association with the world of nature.

185

*Learning to communiciate with plants involves apprecia-
tion and respect.*

To me, the camera has become a way of seeing. Having used one since I was twenty years old and working my way through college with a typewriter and a 4 × 5 Speed Graphic, the camera has become almost an extension of my very being. Rarely am I without it. And if you expect to capture memorable images, neither should you be. The most important things seem to happen when you don't have a camera. But if you always carry one with you, your chances of creating a good photograph are greatly improved.

Most people, certainly those who are nonprofessionals, use a 35mm single-lens reflex (SLR) model. If you own a camera, chances are that's what you have. But if you don't already own one, what kind should you purchase? That's a difficult question to answer, and much depends on how much money you wish to spend. A number of very good 35mm SLR cameras are on the market now, any one of which will do the job. It's best, however, if you avoid buying a little-known brand. Go for the major brands, even if it means spending more. And if you don't have the money to invest—and that's exactly what a camera can be, an investment—then look at good, clean, used cameras. But still hold out for major brand names. You'll be far ahead in the long run. Not only will the camera serve you well because the chances are it has better quality built in; but if you ever decide to sell it, you'll find major brands depreciate far less quickly.

Unless you know someone you can trust at a camera store, don't necessarily rely on what the salespeople have to say. Do your own research. Check the national advertisements to see which brands are sold by the most dealers. And if you purchase used equipment, try to do it only from a reputable camera store or dealer that will give you a basic warranty of sixty to ninety days with a money-back guarantee. If you should buy from an individual, try first to have the camera checked out by a camera repair shop to determine how much is wrong with it. This may not always be possible, of course, and in that case, be aware you're taking your chances. If you decide not to buy through a camera store, check a publication called *Shutterbug Ads*. You may find it at your local library; if not, you may want to subscribe (write to: Box F, Titusville, FL 32780). Advertisers in this publication are claimed to be most reputable, otherwise I'm told the publication will not accept them.

Remember two things in purchasing a camera. First of all, the camera itself is merely a box. It has the capability to hold film and advance it to the next frame. On the other hand, the optics are very important, and that's where you should focus your greatest attention and most money. Second, many SLRs today come loaded with extras. Stay away from them. Keep your camera as simple as possible. The more simple, the less that can go wrong with it. And most of the gadgetry you'll never use, or need, anyway.

Most dealers will offer a discount on camera bodies only. Go for it. Buy the body and then pick up used lenses for it. The standard lens, usually a 50mm, that normally comes with the camera is the most useless lens you'll ever own, especially in working with nature and wildlife. I almost never use mine, except possibly in combination with a bellows or other closeup equipment for shooting tiny wildflowers or insects.

Each year, I teach several nature photographic seminars nationwide, and in those I recommend to my beginning students two lenses: a wide-angle and a short-length telephoto. While they are in training to become professional nature photographers, I'd still recommend the same lenses to anyone wishing to work closely with nature. The wide angle can be anything from a 35mm to a 20mm lens. The telephoto can be anything from a 120mm to a 200mm. Certainly you should not go for a greater focal-length lens than a 300mm, since anything larger most likely will require you to use it on a tripod. If you're into opportunity shots and don't like carrying around any extra weight or more equipment than you absolutely have to, you'll likely want to stay with hand-held equipment.

Going with the equipment, I've mentioned in a major brand (Nikon, Canon, Minolta, Olympus), these lenses may cost you as much as $1,000 to $1,500 new; but if you buy the equipment used, you may get by for $500 to $600. You'll probably want to buy some accessories somewhere along the way, or even other lenses, including a high-powered telephoto. But these two lenses will serve you well, and my only other recommendation for your early efforts would be a closeup attachment, such as a set of extension rings, which will run between $30 and $60 depending upon the brand.

While I don't recommend them for my professional students, the mirror lens (I frown on it because of the fixed *f*-stop), or the zoom lens may work well for the amateur. The optics in the latter have been improved considerably during the past few years until the definition is much more impressive than ever before. With a zoom lens, of course, you can have a combination lens all built within the same package, giving you far greater variety than straight focal-length lenses can offer. A good lens for beginners is one that extends from 35mm to 105mm range, giving you both telephoto and wide-angle capability within the same lens. Sure helps the weight problem, too. The chief advantage of a mirror lens is size and weight, too, as well as cost. You should be able to get a 500 mm mirror lens in a good brand for around $150 to $250, new.

I don't own a mirror lens, nor a zoom, but that's because I shoot professionally. The largest straight focal-length telephoto lens I own is a 300 mm. According to some of my photographer colleagues that's not enough, but it is for me—and it should be for you. If you practice making friends with the creatures you're trying to photograph, or if you employ the techniques we've described in stalking, hiking, or using a blind, you'll be able to get very close to many wild animals to take your shots. You may not get off more than one or two before the noise of the camera itself spooks them, but at least those one or two shots could be very good indeed.

To avoid camera noise, you might like to invest in a muffler, or make one yourself. I've used knitted toboggans or scarves to help muffle the sound of cameras, and it works, but not usually as well as one made to order from the camera store.

Students from Tom Brown's Wilderness Survival &
Tracking School examine plants.

190

A number of good types of film are now on the market, but basically I prefer just one or two—either Kodachrome or Ektachrome. I also recommend slide film over print film. It's cheaper, and offers better results. With the savings in developing costs you soon can buy a projector and screen, or project onto a plain white wall. I once did a public show in Maine on a bed sheet, and it worked very well indeed. Virtually everything published in books and magazines these days is either Kodachrome or Ektachrome, and that ought to be your guide. What the pros use certainly should be good enough for the rest of us. I prefer 64 ASA film, but occasionally go to 200 or 400 ASA. A new 1000 ASA is available now, too, for those extremely poor lighting conditions, or even for indoor photography with available light. It works well but is considerably more grainy than the 64 ASA, which won't make a lot of difference if you're only interested in using it for your own purposes or showing to friends.

Keep in mind that the Kodachrome film tends to have warmer tones and the Ektachrome cooler ones. That is, the overriding color tones in Kodachrome are the yellows and reds, or warm colors; in Ektachrome, the blues and green prevail. Which film you choose is up to you; what is important, however, once you've made your choice, is to stick closely with it. You'll become more familiar with film if you use it all the time, and thus will know what results to expect. Some of the Japanese brands, incidentally, are offering good results, as is Agfachrome, a German film. You might want to try some of those before you settle into one single brand.

If you're photographing in extreme weather conditions, you must take care to protect your film from the elements. That means keeping it dry after exposure. It also means keeping it relatively cool in extremely hot temperatures. Don't, for instance, leave your film, either exposed or unexposed, locked in your car when the thermometer reached 90 or more degrees, and never leave it in direct sunlight.

If you're using your camera in extremely cold conditions (below freezing point), be careful how you advance the film in the camera. Do it slowly and methodically. Under cold conditions, the film is more likely to break in the first place, and secondly, if wound fast, may generate static electricity that creates sparks across the emulsion, which will ruin it and your picture.

When loading the camera, or exchanging film, stand with your shadow over the film, and if the roll is not contained in a cannister as most 35mm SLRs are, keep it tightly rolled. Some of the 2¼ format cameras do not have cannisters, in which case this extra precaution is necessary.

If you've never used a camera before, practice with it before you go into the field. Without film, pretend you're shooting pictures by selecting potential subjects, dissecting them with the eye through the viewfinder, moving in and out, closer and farther away. Learn to manipulate the shutter release easily without looking at it. And when you shoot your pictures, be sure to hold your camera firmly, not allowing it to move about. If you are standing and holding it in your hands, plant your feet firmly about twenty-four inches apart, with all of the foot steady on the ground. Raise the camera to your eye, study your subject, and compose your picture. Then gently and slowly squeeze the shutter release. Don't jerk it—that will cause the camera to move. By gently squeezing the trigger, you'll learn to be much more steady with the camera. As you start to squeeze the shutter release, take a deep breath and hold it. This also helps to steady the camera. Using these techniques will help you as a photographer to harmonize with your environment. You'll less likely clash with it and your sensibility will blend well with those of all other living things.

Once you've learned to manipulate your camera well, then it's time to load the film and go into the field. If you see some wildlife you'd like a picture of, you may want to stalk it. Do so very cautiously. First of all, hopefully you'll already know a few basics about the animal. Do your stalk the same way you would if you had no camera except for one thing: I never approach an animal directly, but at an oblique angle, like a sailboat tacking into the wind.

192

*Knowing specific food plants preferred by animals can
often help you track an animal down.*

193

By moving at oblique angles to the animal, assuming it already knows I'm there, I give the impression I'm not interested in it but am moving on past it, concentrating on another subject somewhere beyond. This often puts animals much more at ease and they'll continue doing whatever it is they're doing. I pause every few steps once I've gotten within camera range, never turning squarely to face my quarry, but just turning my head and camera toward it. I take a picture or two, then move on in the same direction I was going. Or I may turn back on another tack and periodically take other pictures.

Using this method, I've been able to get quite close before the animal spooked and ran away. In some cases, as with grizzly bears, moose, caribou, and even deer, I've gotten to within thirty feet before losing my subject. If I had used better stalking methods, trying to keep the animal from knowing I was about at all, I perhaps could have gotten closer, but the click of the camera, even when muffled, at such close range probably would have given me away.

Many of the stalking techniques discussed earlier will work for you with a camera; others will not work so well. You cannot, for instance, crawl very well with a camera strapped around your neck. And you cannot lie down and still be apt to get good pictures, unless you clearly have an open field of view. So you simply must use your judgement on what will or will not work and adjust your efforts accordingly.

Almost always, a blind will work for you, however, if the creatures you're trying to photograph come to one particular spot such as a water hole or a lush green-grass meadow frequently. In this case, it might be well for you to build a blind and work from it.

When building a blind, try to use materials found on location. Sticks and leaves, weeds and blades of grass can all be interwoven into a very fine blind. Just make sure it's sturdy, allows observation holes and, in this case, camera holes for shots in various directions. Make it as noise-free as possible, so that when you move inside the blind, you'll not likely make any rustling sound or certainly will be able to minimize any other type of sound. If there are no natural materials for use, you may bring in a camouflaged tarp and mount it around posts or sticks securely fastened into the ground. Using a tarp may scare the creatures away for a few days, although if you leave the blind up all the time, they may soon become accustomed to it and pay it no heed at all.

If you're able to drive into wildlife areas, such as some of the wildlife drives provided on refuges owned and administered by the U.S. Fish & Wildlife Service, use your car for a blind. Since animals soon become accustomed to automobiles, you can utilize that for photographing. Always pull to the side of the road, cut the engine, and roll the window down. You may use the car door, or sometimes, depending upon whether you're photographing through the front or back side window, the seat to rest the camera on. Some photographers use a small sandbag set on the door to cushion the camera. I don't, for it seems sand always escapes from the bag somehow and it's one of your camera's worst enemies.

Another good method for photographing certain animals is from a tree stand. The stand should be no more than twenty feet off the ground (fifteen feet usually is sufficient in most cases). Pieces of wood can be nailed into the tree for use as a ladder, but in the interest of not harming the tree, it's better if you fashion a rope ladder with sticks for rungs at intervals. The stand should be no larger than is absolutely necessary for your own comfort, usually about three to four feet square. A half sheet of half-inch-thick plywood works well with a couple of short 2 × 4s nailed under it for support.

It's a good idea to wear camouflage clothing, as we've mentioned earlier, and you should also pay some attention to camouflaging your camera as well. Many cameras have bright silvery lens tubes and sometimes shiny bodies, too. The muffler, if you're using one, should be of drab olive material, which will solve your camouflage problem as well as silencing the camera. Otherwise, it may be necessary to sew a camouflage covering for the camera or lens. Or you can just take

195

your chances, as I often do, and hope the animals won't mind anyway.

Two primary elements the photographer, whether amateur or professional, must become aware of: light and motion. And the greater of these is light. Photography itself is a coined Greek work meaning "writing with light." And that's exactly what it is—creating an image with light. Light is the single most important ingredient of all natural elements in creating a good photograph.

While most of the SLR 35mm cameras have a built-in light meter, which will help immensely in getting the right exposure for your picture, try not to rely upon it entirely. Learn to judge light with the eye. I preach this more often than any other single factor in my professional photography seminars. Only by developing an eye for light and the role it plays upon your subject will you become a better than average photographer. Study light. Use your light meter as a guide, but to ensure good shots, bracket your shots, taking one at an f-stop or two below what the meter indicates and one at a stop or two above. Test it with your eyes open only a slit and determine, under those conditions, where the dark areas are and the ones more directly in natural light. Check your local public library for books dealing with art subjects that pay special attention to light. But most of all, learn to recognize it in the field.

There are exceptions, of course, but generally speaking the best lighting is morning light, defined as anywhere between fifteen minutes before sunrise and 9 A.M. The next best time to photograph from an ideal lighting standpoint is from 4 P.M. to thirty minutes before dusk. Midday is not, normally, a good time, but again this depends upon cloud cover and where you're working.

When photographing in a woodland, I prefer foggy or light rainy days. As long as there's high overcast, I get the kind of light that brings out the life of the woodland. The wetness of the rain gives luster to the leaves, the water may bead on their tips or, in the case of a pine forest, on the tips of the needles, turning it into a magic fairyland. The lighting is more

196

Knowing plants preferred for nesting is another way of finding animals.

uniform in a woodland on an overcast or rainy day, too. You don't have to worry about those dark shady spots nor those unattractive hot spots. Most color films today have a latitude to help handle variations in lighting, but these are too extreme for most films.

Moisture can be very important in color photography, even when photographing animals. Often it creates an aura or mood in the foliage and around the entire scene, making the animals you photograph stand out even better than they normally would. Some of the finest mood shots I've ever seen have been taken on foggy mornings. Sometimes photogra-

197

phers carry moisturizers for use with plants, wildflowers, or even spiderwebs and some insects, spraying the subject with water before taking pictures. I seldom do this myself, preferring instead to work with nature as I find it. If you do decide to use one, however, just go to a hardware or variety store and buy a little spraycan moisturizer—the type used to dampen clothes for ironing or for spraying a mist on indoor potted plants—and it will work fine.

The other major ingredient I consider important is movement, or motion. If the subject is moving, how much it is moving, and how fast? That's going to play a role in deciding how fast to set your shutter speed. If you want to freeze the action in place, you may have to go to a faster shutter speed. And if you do that, how much will it affect the amount of light coming into the camera? The light meter will help you to determine that. Normally, it's rare in working with many animals that you'd need to consider a greater shutter speed than 1/250th of a second, and most likely not more than 1/125th of a second. You may want to go slower, too, but it may not be possible for you to steady the lens, unless you're exceptionally good at it, at speeds under 1/60th of a second. And most assuredly is you're using a telephoto lens.

When capturing images of wildlife, or of nature, don't by any means limit yourself to the wildlife alone. Take shots of footprints, plants, scenery, signs, and any related activities. The camera not only is valuable for capturing those beautiful images but also as a tool for documenting data. The pictures will provide proof of what you saw, and you may sharpen your outdoor skills by studying them long after you've returned home from your outdoor adventure.

Once you've reached a degree of proficiency at taking pictures on the land, you may want to broaden your field to include underwater or aerial photography. Working under water will require some additional gear, but you can perform excellent aerial photography with some of the equipment we've discussed here. Even the underwater portions are much simpler than you may think.

198

When I first decided to try underwater photography, I had a friend at a nearby university lab workshop make up a Plexiglass box about eighteen inches deep with sealed seams. I placed my regular camera inside it—making sure to keep the lens pressed right against the glass to avoid reflections—estimated the focus, and, walking my camera and box around the edge of a small lake, took pictures among the roots and underwater portions of cattails. Once I felt comfortable with this, I donned a mask and snorkel so I could see under water myself. I noticed many of the bluegill fish and occasionally a largemouth bass would become curious enough to venture close to the box. And I snapped pictures of them, using only natural light. They came out well.

Later, on a trip to the Florida Keys, I began to use the box in shallow water on the mudflats. It was surprising what I could get from the box. But by this time I had become hooked, and soon I purchased my first underwater camera, a Nikonos III, and an underwater flash and filter set. Filters are necessary if you get very far under water—more than about two to three feet, and maybe even then, depending upon the water quality. But you can photograph within the upper two to three feet in good clear water using only a snorkel and a simple underwater camera. And you can get some good pictures. I haven't taken up diving yet, and probably won't. Whether you decide to or not is entirely up to you. If you do and you're in the right places, such as the great coral reef on the ocean side of the Florida Keys, you may get some excellent images of all kinds of creatures of the deep that come there to feed and play among the living coral.

If you decide to do some photography from an airplane of wildlife, it can work particularly well with larger groups of animals or birds. If you're chartering an aircraft, rent a plane that is small and can be slowed to speeds well under 85 mph. The slower the better. I like the Cessna 150 really well because it's a two-seater, allowing you to sit alongside the pilot and communicate easily with him. Secondly, the window on this plane opens from the bottom, and, once released, flies up against the

Appreciating plants brings you into contact with the smaller creatures of the earth, such as this Golden Orb spider.

overhead wing, allowing you plenty of space to put your camera outside the window. Use an infinity focal setting, of course, and you'll need a lens that will allow you to photograph without getting the wing struts or wheels of the plane in the picture. Also beware of the prop wash. Unless you shoot at extremely fast shutter speeds, the prop wash may turn up in your pictures. I recommend at least 1/250th or 1/500th of a second (most likely the latter) to avoid this. Even then, the light will sometimes catch the prop wash just right and show up in the images.

You may ask the pilot to fly as low as you feel the need and he feels he can safely handle. In areas where the air is stable, I've flown at altitudes of no more than fifty feet to capture flocks of common egrets and great blue heron, spoonbills and white ibis in the Florida Everglades. (Be sure to check the regulations in national parks and wildlife refuges; most have minimum altitude requirements.) A pilot friend of mine in Alaska who owns his own Piper Super Cub says he's flown among migrating caribou herds so close to the ground the herds would part in front of the plane. "It's like being a part of them," he said. Naturally that would permit too close a range for good photography, for you would not be able to show the herd in proper perspective. He did it not for photography but for biological research, which required close inspection of the animals. Be aware always of creating undue stress upon the wildlife you are photographing, however.

Aerial photography works well over water, too, where you may have sharks, porpoises, or whales close to the surface. I've been able to capture spectacular shots of migrating gray whales off southern California and Baja. And I've worked with hammerhead sharks—whole schools of them—near Dry Tortugas seventy miles beyond Key West in the Gulf of Mexico. Occasionally, I've worked with migrating birds, especially Canada geese, photographing them flying alongside not more than fifty feet off the wingtip. But this doesn't work too well for more than a couple of shots, for the geese try to avoid the plane and veer away very quickly.

201

Getting good wildlife photographs requires great patience, of course, same as it does for observation. Getting to know and understand the other creatures, developing the oneness-of-life attitude is not easy, nor does it come quickly. Even then, one must be adept and quick at taking pictures in order to capture the kind of impressive shots that will become conversation pieces. But it is fun—and most rewarding.

Chapter 12

Training

I have often wondered, if animals *could* talk—if they could verbalize in terminology we humans could understand—who would listen? After all, there's considerable evidence we don't listen even to other humans. Imagine what it would be like if we added to this stream of vocalization the sounds of all the animals we know.

Well, fact is, some animals do talk, but thus far they've had little to say beyond very basic words or phrases. One, a talking harbor seal named Hoover at the New England Aquarium in Boston, even makes complete statements, such as "Hello there," or "Come over here," and sometimes, when he's had enough of baffling humans with conversation, simply "Get lost."

By so doing, Hoover is believed to be the only animal on earth that has learned to mimic such human sounds, although there's another harbor seal named Salisbury at the New England Aquarium who can manage a "hello."

Hoover, named after the vacuum cleaner because he started to eat like one during his younger days, was reared by George and Alice Swallow of Cundys Harbor, Maine, after

Alice's brother found the infant seal on the beach. The mother had been shot by a fisherman, so the Swallows became Hoover's surrogate parents. When he refused a bottle of milk, they mashed up mackerel in a meat grinder and force-fed him. "That's when he started to act like a vacuum cleaner," Mrs. Swallow said, "so we named him after one."

Hoover grew up to be a neighborhood pet and, as he got older and larger, the children would take him riding in a wheelbarrow. No one ever made any attempt to get him to talk, but Mr. Swallow said he did holler at the seal a lot—things like "Come over here," and "Get outa here," some of the same expressions that Hoover uses today.

The Swallows never noticed him doing much beyond making garbled noises in his throat until one day Mr. Swallow said, "Hello there," and the seal responded, "Hello there." "I wasn't sure I'd heard right," Mr. Swallow recalled, "but after a while, I asked him his name and he replied 'Hoover.'" "When we took him to the aquarium—we hated to do it, but he was eating us out of house and home (seventy dollars' worth of fish a week)—I told the fellow rather sheepishly there I thought he could talk, but he gave me such a strange look I never mentioned it again."

In a few cases, dolphins also have been reported to have pronounced certain words, and in 1973, *Behavior,* a scholarly Dutch journal, mentioned two porpoises that had imitated the movements of human beings. One such act involved a baby porpoise in an aquarium who was fascinated by people passing by outside. Once a smoker, noting the porpoise, blew smoke toward it. The porpoise went to its mother, got a mouthful of milk, came back, and blew the milk at the smoker. In the water, the milk dispersed and appeared almost like smoke. On another occasion, an adult porpoise in captivity became fascinated with a diver who periodically entered to clean the tank with a large vacuum. It watched while the diver used a rag to clean a viewing window. Later, the porpoise used a flipper to rub the same window, emitting bursts of bubbles to the surface as the diver had done.

Animals that have learned to do simple mimicking or vo-

Sea mammals seem to enjoy being trained at the Miami Seaquarium.

calizations have often learned through some form of training. But the fact that animals do not talk in human sounds doesn't mean they don't talk. Eminent psychologist Dr. John Lilly, who for years worked with numerous creatures and most specifically with dolphins, approached the matter from a totally different aspect. He attempted to build a computer system through which humans could establish communication with dolphins on their level and using their sounds. Dr. Lilly found it very difficult to do, however, for he believes the dolphin intelligence level far surpasses that of man.

"The highest intelligence on the planet," Lilly once said,

"probably exists in the sperm whale, who has a brain weighing some ten thousand grams, six times larger than that of an average human brain. I'm convinced," he added, "that intelligence is a function of absolute brain size." Man, Lilly believes, is naturally hampered in developing greater intelligence simply because his brain is not large enough and because his genetic skeletal structure prohibits any expansion in its size. "Maybe the human brain can evolve further if we get control of our genetic code."

Aside from Lilly's observation, there is considerable evidence that many animals do indeed possess great intelligence, and moreover that we as humans may be able to learn from them. A good part of the focus of this book and its raison d'être is to help people begin to better interpret other life forms on the planet. In order to understand some of that world, I turned to trainers and keepers in zoos and aquariums, places where creatures of the wild have been put on display for the purpose of close public viewing and, in some cases, educational entertainment.

In most every case, I found the greatest training, and hence communication, has taken place using a concept long ago prescribed by noted animal behaviorist B. F. Skinner: positive reinforcement, or operant conditioning. Joan Caron, chief trainer at the Miami Seaquarium, believes there may be no limit to developing a communication system with killer whales and dolphins, the two principal marine animals with which she is involved. But like Dr. Lilly, she does not believe it will actually happen—more because of the inability of humans to pursue the matter than because of the receptivity or capability of the animals involved. Already some aquariums have achieved remarkable results with their charges from the wild animal world.

Lou Roth, who handles whale training at Miami Seaquarium, demonstrated for me some of what he's able to do with a killer whale. Using only body English for communication, Roth dived into the killer whale tank, to be picked up on the back of the whale and, while firmly grasping the dorsal fin, taken on a spiraling, roller-coaster ride that kept him under water nearly half the time. It was obvious both Roth and the whale loved it.

Another act which Roth does with the whale during the public demonstrations features him sitting on the whale's nose while it leaps vertically more than twenty feet into the air to touch a ball suspended overhead.

Does it take long to train a killer whale to engage in such tactics on command? "Not long at all," said Roth. "Sometimes we've introduced a new act, run through it a couple of times, and let the whale think on it overnight. The next day it comes off perfectly. Perhaps it's not even necessary to give them time to think on it. Probably they have the ability to do the act perfectly five minutes later. But we give them time to think about the act, and then we do it."

In similar fashion, Dr. Dale Woodyard of Windsor University in Canada is making animal behavior history working with the manatee, one of North America's endangered species, a stone's throw away from Miami Seaquarium. "There is evidence," he says, "that we cannot only communicate with manatee, but that they can learn to carry out some of our wishes." After a few short weeks of research, Woodyard was able to get some of the manatees to respond to certain body signals he gives them. "And when they don't do it right," he says, "it's obvious they grow frustrated because they know they haven't done it right."

Of course, trainers in general agree it's much easier to work with an animal that has been born and bred in captivity and is accustomed to being around humans from the outset. Tim Desmond, assistant curator for mammals training at Marineland in Southern California, has experienced considerable differences in animals brought in from the wilds and those born at Marineland. A trained psychologist, Desmond says there's a natural period of adjustment which must occur before any real training can take place. "If the animal is unhappy or has a problem, we must overcome or resolve that problem. A big one for the wild creature, of course, is confinement and change of environment. That takes a considerable period of readjustment. Sometimes, it never entirely happens. The

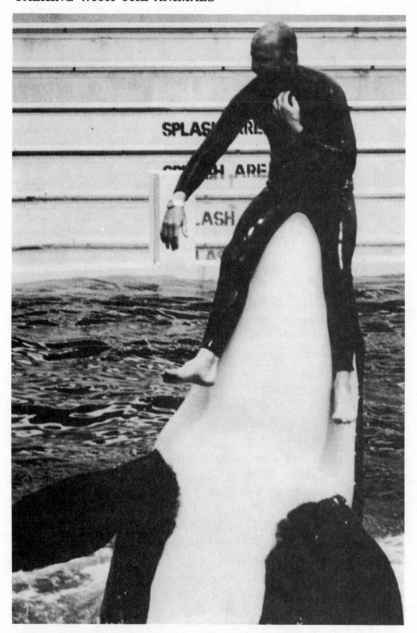

Lou Roth, head whale trainer, goes through exercises with one of his charges at the Miami Seaquarium.

spirit of the animal from the wild is often still there in the wild the remainder of its life."

When a show is staged for the public at Marineland, Desmond often is in an enclosure backstage where he can easily observe the reactions of the killer whales to the trainers putting on the show. And he's constantly advising and consulting with the performers based on the readings he's getting from the two killer whales—Orky and Corky—in the tank below, all while the show is in progress.

"In many ways," he said, chuckling, "they're like big, playful children. We know they can do what they darn well please. You don't argue with a creature that is several times your size and can merely swim away if it doesn't want to do something. And they're always testing you, reading you and sometimes taking you right to the brink of your patience level. They know what they're doing and they know you know what their options are, too."

Tim Desmond and Joan Caron, a continent apart, both share a fascination with the animals with which they work and both think that we, as humans, have a great deal more to learn about the animals than they do about us. Both firmly believe the reason wild creatures are much harder to train is simply because they mistrust humans. "They are naturally suspicious of humans because of what they've experienced from us for centuries," says Desmond. "Man has through the ages been a natural enemy to most animals in the wild. And you can't erase overnight that wariness which has become so inbred for centuries and generation after generation in the animal world."

The existence of that natural wall of defense between wildlife and man was demonstrated in some most unusual studies performed in 1982 by Dr. Betsy Smith of Florida International University at Miami, utilizing dolphins and autistic children. Soon after initiating the program, Dr. Smith observed distinct changes in both the autistic children with whom she was working and the dolphins. Carolyn Brooks, of Key Largo, Florida, a psychologist trained in play therapy who assisted Dr. Smith, says the dolphins showed a definite

209

The whale seems to enjoy the show as much as the audience does.

difference in attitude toward the autistic children than they had shown toward other humans. Both she and Dr. Smith believe it to be because the dolphins are able to read signals from us and because autistic children do not possess any inbred bias toward other creatures. "They operate on an easy-to-understand, basic level, a symbolism that is more universal in other life forms."

Dr. Lilly in California goes even further, claiming that dolphins have a very high-frequency sonar with which they can inspect something and look at its internal structure. There's some feeling that other animal species may also possess similar abilities in reading an individual person. It may be such communication, for instance, that allows the grizzly bear in Alaska to know the difference between a human who would not harm it and a human who carries a gun, even though the gun may be concealed. And it may make a difference in the amount of confidence anyone is able to build with another creature in the realm of observation or rapport. Years ago, a psychologist friend advised me to think only positive thoughts about creatures with which I hoped to establish an intimate relationship. It works with people and I feel, after a quarter century of experience, it works with animals.

The training of all types of animals apparently has one particular prerequisite to reaching success: The animals must be content, happy, and trusting. Several notable examples of other creatures being trained to work with or for humans have been documented around the world. The dolphin therapy with autistic children practiced by Dr. Smith in southern Florida is but one of many studies in which animals are used effectively to communicate and to bring about an improved attitude, setting the stage for learning processes among mentally handicapped people.

In one case of Dr. Smith's which involved a boy named Michael Williams, a few weeks of carefully supervised dolphin therapy brought such remarkable improvements in Michael's overall attitude that he began talking. Previously he had uttered only gutteral sounds and used certain body motions as means of communication.

During one session, described by Dr. Smith in a paper she prepared for delivery at the French animal research association's annual meeting in 1982 in Paris, Michael actually fed the dolphins fish. At first, Dr. Smith gave Michael a few herring and he merely threw them in the water, but later he twice presented an individual fish to an individual dolphin.

"As we ended the session that day," she continued, "Michael stood at the beginning of the dock and stared directly at one dolphin, Little Bit, who lay on his side with one eye looking directly into Michael's eyes. They both stayed in this position, silent, for about three minutes. Then the other dolphins came to the dock, splashing and playing, and Little Bit broke off the contact. Michael then turned and went to the car."

211

Bear yearning for honey at the Bronx Zoo, New York.

Dr. Smith said she has strong beliefs, partially as a result of her work with dolphins and autistic persons, that even language may be produced in "non-verbal" children. "If the dolphin, through his constant insistent play, can establish a rapport with the autistic child, it is conceivable that the child can develop self-initiated play activity. This could possibly open the pathways at the proper moment," she added, "for a peak performance to take place, a pathway that would allow meaning to be attached to previously garbled patterns.

"Water can be felt and tasted as water; the dolphin becomes the dolphin; swimming, touching, feelings become part of a common experience. The dolphin, because of its isolation from normal people may be able to trigger that first step of spontaneous activity in the isolated child. This could provide us with a possibility of connecting the child to our symbolic universe through the mind of the dolphin."

After a few weeks of dolphin therapy, Michael's attitude changed from one of uncommunicative indifference to one of smiles, relaxation, and affectionate reaching out to other individuals as well as to the dolphins. Previously filled with numerous fears of various aspects of his environment, including open spaces, movement, and so on, he miraculously lost almost all of those fears after being introduced to the dolphins. He began not only observing but interacting with the dolphins and people around him.

"When a normal person engages in water play with dolphins or swims with them," Dr. Smith explains, "he brings into the water many behaviors that inhibit his ability to make contact with the dolphin. There is the question of his confidence in the foreign involvement, and his needs and expectation of dolphin behavior vis-a-vis his learned hierarchical relationship with animals."

Perhaps the researcher G. Bateson put it most succinctly in his book *Mind in the Waters,* when he said:

> I think there is something very important for people who are swimming with porpoises to know; and that is, that certainly when you are in the water with a porpoise, you

213

are not in the position you are with a dog or cat. A dog or cat takes a filial position with you, puts you in the position of parent or leader or whatever, and you get all the begging for food, and so on, that dogs and cats do. You don't do that when you are in the water with a porpoise, because you are the child and the porpoise is the parent. Now, if you are the swimmer and you can accept being the child and let the porpoise teach you, there is a lot you can learn about an animal by raising it, by becoming its parent. But then you are in a false situation, you are doing the leading. If you let the animal do the teaching, you will find out a lot more about the animal.

With certain creatures, some observers believe no teaching takes place. William (Bill) Haast, who has operated the Miami Serpentarium for more than twenty years and worked with snakes in a laboratory situation all of that time, says he is convinced that snakes are born with all the knowledge they will ever have. "Snakes do not have to learn," he said. "They are fully equipped to deal with any situation the day they are born. I've observed cobras many times, and I'm convinced their minds are as fully developed the day they are born as the day they die. Theirs is not a learned behavior."

Training the incarcerated wild animal might be a lot easier, some behaviorists believe, if the animal were made to feel it was still in the wild. Some zoos are now doing just that. In time past, animals were strictly confined; the cage may have been a little square, or a little perch or a rock where the animal was the focal point of the exhibit with not much else to do but go crazy. Hopefully, such times are gone forever. Animal keepers today, with few exceptions, pay more attention to the creature's physical and psychological needs. It used to be a common goal just to keep the creature alive. No more.

Dr. Inga Poglayen, former curator of birds and mammals at the Arizona-Sonora Desert Museum in Tucson, believes this change in attitude is due in large part to the increasing demand for zoos to breed rare animals in capitivity. "Over the years," she says, "zoos have found out they need to breed ani-

Bear trying to retrieve honey from a mechanical honey tree at the Bronx Zoo, New York.

215

mals. But you can only get them to reproduce when they're content. A content animal will mate, then raise its young."

Dr. Howard Lawler, curator of reptiles and small animals at the Desert Museum, believes the incarceration of any animal brings moral and ethical responsibility: "I feel when we incarcerate any animal, be it an invertebrate on up to man, we take upon ourselves the responsibility to provide the fundamental requirements for that organism. I think along with that, when we talk about animals below humans, we also have to consider their psychological requirements. Because we have taken the creature out of its natural environment which permits a free-living natural state and imposed certain limitations on it, we are morally bound to look out for its welfare."

Lawler further suggests that in many cases, particularly with smaller animals and reptiles, conditions imposed may be so unrestrictive that the incarcerated creature is indeed unaware it's in captivity. "That's what those of us who are keepers of creatures from the wild animal world must strive to do nowadays," Lawler adds. "We may never reach that point totally, but we can certainly try."

Many zoo keepers, handlers, and trainers share the belief that the biggest stress factor for incarcerated animals is boredom. Dr. Poglayen points out that they no longer have to go hunting for their food; they get it at four o'clock, regularly. Their water is already there so they don't have to go searching for it. They have no predators, so they let down their defenses. And they have nothing to do, so they sit there, bored. They start pulling fur. They start pacing. How many times have you visited zoo animals and watched while they pace back and forth, hour after hour after hour. Bears, lions, tigers—many creatures do this because there's simply nothing else to do. They are bored out of their skulls.

Karen Pryor, a consultant on animal behavior, once reported being called upon to install a program at the National Zoo. Theodore Reed, then director of the zoo, mentioned such specific behavioral problems as polar bears that banged on their steel doors hour after hour; giraffes that sometimes refused to go indoors before a cold snap and had to be chased

216

about by ten men with sticks; and a chimp that sat in the corner all day plucking the hair out of its arms.

Reed was not just worried about boredom among the animals—he was worried about boredom among the keepers as well. But Pryor soon taught the keepers to take a greater interest in the animals' welfare and, by using a system of positive reinforcement and affection training, to lift the animals out of their state of boredom.

Training, of course, is time-consuming. It takes patience and more patience. Some keepers simply did not have time to spend training the animals, so they were given extra help. Some curators became exasperated. "I do not see the value," said one curator, "in training the panda to stand on its head to impress the other keepers." The value, of course, as Pryor pointed out, was in the process, not the product; the trainer was learning to train and the animal was no longer bored. Within weeks, keepers began to report phenomenal progress. One trainer had even trained a chinchilla to weigh itself by hopping into a basket which could then be put on a scale—a big improvement over chasing it all over the cage with a net to catch and weigh it.

The National Zoo was not alone. Zoos all over the country are getting a new look. The Bronx Zoo installed honey trees for its bears, but the bears had to work to get the honey out, and the visitors enjoyed their behavior even more. The San Diego Wild Animal Park conditioned several species of wild birds, utilizing positive reinforcement, to exhibit natural behavior to the public.

The Brookfield Zoo near Chicago, like the Bronx Zoo, has experimented with extensive automated exhibits that allow animals to develop a natural behavior such as hunting, stalking or, as in the bears' case, merely reaching up and licking the honey from the automated honey tree.

Training animals to react to love and affection, or sometimes for food treats, can be very important. At the National Zoo, for instance, a polar bear broke a canine tooth, which called for veterinary attention. The tooth could get infected and develop into a serious illness. Customarily, a bear of this

217

*Some wild animals, such as these Key deer in Florida,
can be encouraged with salt licks or other food.*

stature would require being shot with a tranquilizer gun with a stiff dosage that might be harmful to its life. But within a few days, the keeper had taught the bear to stick its nose out through a slot in the door and allow its lip to be lifted. When that behavior was shaped, they called in the vet, the trainer signaled the bear, it poked its nose out, and the vet inspected the tooth. It was all done with raisins.

Other natural methods of eliminating boredom may be used. In the Phoenix Zoo, the great apes are given branches and palm fronds on a daily basis. They also receive telephone books. Tearing out the pages gives them something to do and provides them with nesting material. Natural furniture such as the fronds and branches are also given to birds that demonstrate neurotic behavior. Food for the orangutans is spread all over the impoundment, and keepers even hide some of it so the creatures must search to find it. Keeper Joni Stimson says this stimulates them to act more as if they're in their natural environment in the wild. "It gives them something to do throughout the morning so they don't wolf down their food and then sit bored stiff the rest of the day."

Stimson, who is responsible for the elephants as well, has taught them a routine which involves rolling logs with their trunks, stepping over obstacles, and jogging around the circumference of their compound. The elephants look forward to their exercise routine. "When you're working an animal and he's vocalizing, squeaking," she said, "you sense he's relatively happy with what's going on. I have seen depressed elephants. They just stand and rock their heads back and forth."

Animals, if properly stimulated, soon learn to react to people, and that in itself keeps them from getting bored. An elephant named Ruby once carried a small log around with her as kind of a security blanket. At night, when the keepers had all gone home, Ruby would wait for the security guard to drive by on his route, and she'd then toss the log in front of his truck so he'd have to stop and give it back to her. It's the same reaction you may have experienced with your family dog who often will grab a stick in its mouth and bring it to you. If you try to take it, the dog will sometimes hang on, wanting to wrestle with you. And if you get the stick and don't throw it, the dog is disappointed. But by throwing the stick and watching the dog go after it, you have initiated and are participating in a game, a game that wards off boredom for the dog. It's the same for the elephant.

We can learn much from observing zoo animals and trained ones in aquariums and other public exhibits, but we must open our minds as we observe. Howard Lawler points out that lizards doing head bobs and pushups are essentially engaging in a form of nonverbal communication that has just as much significance among the lizards as conversation does among us. But we have to understand it as such, and we have to open our minds to it.

More and more, zoos are becoming the final domain of several endangered species. The California condor, it would seem, may soon be found no more in the wild, but they are beginning to reproduce in the San Diego Zoo's Wild Animal Park. Continued success at maintaining a species for generations depends a great deal on the keepers' ability to keep the creatures happy and contented. Psychological attitude, it has been proven beyond doubt, has a definite bearing not only on reproduction, but on sustaining life itself. A creature bored into a state of depression, B. F. Skinner once said, is more susceptible to disease simply because it gives up the will to live.

In numerous instances, animals have been taught to work, to perform skills that would be difficult or, in some cases, nearly impossible for humans. Pigeons, rats, and dolphins have most often been the subjects of work experiments. (Apparently, the idea is not new. Ancient cave and tomb paintings show wild animals being utilized in work situations.)

Since the 1950s, researchers have tried to persuade industry to use pigeons in place of humans in some tedious assembly-line inspection jobs. For example, people hired to inspect drug capsules for defects make errors about 15 percent of the time, but pigeons used in the same task have a rate of only 1 percent error. Dr. Thom Verhave, who conducted the experiment for a pharmaceutical company, said the pigeons

Brown pelicans, though an endangered species, allow humans to come close at many Florida docks.

were accurate 99 percent of the time after only a week of training. In another experiment, pigeons were used to inspect electrical diodes for defects; and George Fournier, a Boston psychologist, is now working on training birds to spot blemishes on giant rolls of paper, as well as streaks and grain in photographic film. In England, blood samples are being flown to labs via carrier pigeons. To hire a taxi to do the job would cost $3 to $5 and take up to twenty minutes, but the birds do it in less than five minutes and cost only pennies per day to maintain.

In Boston, a young man paralyzed from the shoulders down uses a capuchin monkey named Hellion to do his household chores. Hellion removes food from the refrigerator, feeds her disabled master, turns lights on and off, puts cassettes into a tape recorder, and brushes his hair.

The Navy in San Diego has trained porpoises to carry tools to scientists in an underwater research station, and is using sea lions to retrieve or deliver objects at great depths. The sea lions have recovered anti-submarine test rockets at depths of nearly five hundred feet. In another project, a killer whale recovered dummy torpedoes for the Navy from a depth of 1,600 feet in the ocean. A few years ago, the Israelis were using fish armed with radio signal devices to spy on the underwater movements of ships and submarines.

Dr. Raymond Nolan of the U.S. Army has taught rats to sniff out land mines by associating the smell of TNT with pleasurable brain stimulation. He trained the rats by inserting electrodes into an area near the hypothalamus, the brain's pleasure center. The electrodes deliver a highly rewarding stimulation whenever the rats press a treadle bar. But the rats only had access to the bar when TNT vapors were present. Nolan also monitored their brain waves on a computer. Hooked into microcomputers, the rats going into the field in search of pleasurable TNT odors, upon finding their target, would automatically relay messages on the computer. That would give monitors the exact location of each mine, and they could then be retrieved without loss of life. In the past mines

222

Swans and other wild water birds will often approach when food is thrown into the water.

have been recovered by foot soldiers carrying electromagnetic detectors.

Humanists have voiced some concern about the ethics of having animals, particularly animals that are truly from the wild and not bred for domesticity, do such work, and they may have strong grounds for their objections. But in most cases where animals have been trained to work, it's apparent that the animals enjoy what they are doing. Which proves these animals may not be so closely related to man after all.

Chapter 13

"Ask now the beasts, and they shall teach thee"
—Job XII 7:7

In past chapters, we've discussed methods and given examples of how we as humans might better come to understand other forms of life—plant, insect, and animal. We've talked about the need to develop a frame of mind conducive to entering their world, how we can not only gain their confidence but actually move, physically and mentally, within their realm of existence. Now, in this final chapter, we need to examine the future. Just where do we go from here? What can animals teach us? And what can we teach them?

These are important questions, filled with challenging overtones. They are questions that may or may not be answered by the scientific world, but instead perhaps by the individual through his or her own intimate experiences. The answers may never fall within the realm of public domain, but live merely in the collective memories of those who experience them. Encounters with other life forms, in many ways, are very private happenings.

Before we look at the future, it is only fitting that we study the past. The past, after all, is the catalyst for the future; without rooting ourselves in history, we can never hope to give ourselves direction for the years ahead. Other forms of life have been so much a part of our past, perhaps even more than we realize, from the earliest times. Even the Bible speaks of the beginning as "the Word." One might speculate that the word—and thus, in a sense, the beginning—was the name of an animal.

One of the earliest known books, written in ancient Sanskrit, was *The Panchatantra,* which dealt with animals and animal life. It contained five collections of animal fables that formed the basis for most Hindu mythology. This was the forerunner of a period of ancient literature that ultimately developed into the Book of Revelations.

The Egyptians, ancient Greeks, and Romans all perpetrated stories of animals from the distant frontiers of their empires. Thus animals became very much a part of early civilizations—even though some of them existed only in the imagination. Early Christians invented monster animals and told stories about them designed as a means of mind control. By instilling fear in their followers they were able to maintain better discipline. That same correlation was used in the Bible and has been carried down to this day. The serpent, or snake, definitely has three strikes against it simply because of all the undeserved publicity it has received in Scripture. This has had an impact upon the lives of snakes, too; for many people throughout the world today, the only good snake is a dead one.

Later, science fiction picked up on the animal world, creating monsters far beyond the imagination of most humans. And so it continues to this day.

226

An alligator in Okeefenokee Swamp, an animal making a comeback under protective legislation.

In many instances, animals have been elevated to human status. As a result, we have come to think of them as just human-type creatures in another form. Consider the impact that Walt Disney had upon the world of animals. Animal fables existed in Aesop's day, of course, but they live on still in the form of cartoons. And then there are such popular books as *The Day of the Dolphins* and *Jonathan Livingston Seagull,* which influence our society in a more realistic way.

Little doubt remains today that animals do indeed possess intelligence, that they can and do, in many instances, use powers of reasoning. Indeed, researchers who have spent years working closely with certain biological species claim that some are more intelligent than we are.

In the beginning, early man lived by the natural laws of

227

his world. His environment dictated the way in which he lived, the food he ate, where he slept, the places to which he traveled. But as he gained knowledge and began to "improve" his lifestyle, he removed himself more and more from the natural laws that governed his life. In place of these natural laws, he created for himself a set of moral values. At first, many of those moral values were no doubt closely aligned with the natural laws. But over a period of centuries, as generation after generation passed, the moral code lost its correlation with the natural world or the natural laws that governed that world.

This "separateness" led to our belief that we are indeed different from all other forms of life. And not only different but better. That is why we think of animals as being not only inferior to man but part of man's domain. They are ours to manipulate, to manage, to use as we see fit. Only in very recent times have animals and other life forms been assigned rights. When we wanted something, we took it, even if it destroyed the final remaining habitat in a specific area for one animal or an entire colony of animals.

I remember a few years ago a large tract of sand dunes near a beach in St. Petersburg, Florida, being leveled for a golf course, although the area had been a nesting area for hundreds of laughing gulls, perhaps for several centuries. Environmentalists (the name assigned to those who profess to care about our world, including the creatures with which we cohabit the planet) raised a furor which delayed construction of the golf course for several months. In the end, however, the world had another golf course, and the laughing gulls were forced to abandon their traditional nesting area. Now, instead of the cries of thousands of sea gulls carried aloft by ocean winds, there are the shouts and laughter of golfers. The city needed another golf course; it could do without laughing gulls.

In many instances, it has suited our purpose to ignore the existence of other life forms; or, if we did acknowledge their existence, to ill consider their needs, desires, or hopes. We have no way of knowing if other life forms do indeed hope or dream, but neither do we know that they don't. Until we can

228

be certain they do not, why not give them the benefit of the doubt?

As long as we tend to consider ourselves the center of the universe, with everything else revolving around us, it is not likely we're ever going to assign any real importance to other forms of life. Even the methods by which we measure intelligence are based on our own preconceptions. Just what is this thing called intelligence in the first place? Is it related to learning? And what is learning? Dr. Howard Lawler of the Arizona-Sonora Desert Museum asked me that question when I confronted him with Bill Haast's proposition that snakes do not learn, that they possess all their knowledge from birth. Is a conditioned response learning? Or is learning the process by which we bring together certain responses, stimuli, knowledge already attained and direct it toward achieving something we did not know before, or had not accomplished before?

The fact is, few psychologists or behaviorists can agree even among themselves on an operational definition for intelligence, or learning. "Defining intelligence," observed one, "has never worked well with people. It's utterly hopeless with animals." All too often, it's measured in humans by a so-called intelligence test—the Stanford-Binet I.Q. test, based upon a known environment and data acquired or taught in schools. If we choose members of the same population on which the original test items were validated, middle-class American whites, the test is useful for predicting academic success among members of this particular group. Culture plays an important role here. A five-year-old child might be asked to describe a TV set, for instance. But if the child were raised in a part of the world where TV sets did not exist, this information would be totally foreign and the child would flunk that portion of the test.

By the same principle, intelligence in biological life forms cannot be adequately measured either. And no two biological species of creatures could be given the same test, anyway. Lifestyles vary so much that it would be virtually impossible

Are we so superior that animals have nothing to teach us? This ptarmigan was photographed in Alaska.

to reach a standard of measurement in applying such a test result.

Many of the encounters I've experienced with wild animals have shown me, without doubt, that animals do think, that they do, in a number of instances, exercise reasoning power; and while their environments are distinctly different from our own, who is to say that they are not as intelligent in their ways as we are in ours? When I think about animals responding to certain conditions, I am reminded of the story of a man in Pennsylvania, whom we'll call Joe, who owned a large dog. Year after year, when Joe and his wife went on vacation, he took his dog with him. Then one year Joe decided to leave the dog at a nearby kennel while they went on vacation alone. When they returned, the dog was obviously sulking. At home that night, when Joe in customary fashion took off his shoes and set them by his favorite TV chair, the dog came over, sniffed them, and then urinated in them. It was clearly a sign of displeasure, a vivid expression of how the dog felt about being left behind while his master went on vacation.

Rockefeller University professor Donald R. Griffin, whose research in the field of animal behavior resulted in a book called *Animal Thinking* (published in 1984 by Harvard University Press), says people are taught that it's unscientific to ask what an animal thinks or feels. Such questions from students, he says, are often actively discouraged, ridiculed, and treated sometimes with open hostility. Griffin does believe in the ability of other forms to think and offers a number of suggestions to back up his points. "We can investigate animal minds," he says, "by measuring brain waves and eye movements to determine whether animals dream. More and more, ethologists are finding animals that behave as though they could foresee the outcome of their action."

He relates in his book an example of a green heron that takes bread from a picnic table and strews it on the surface of a nearby creek in order to snag fish that rise to the bait. I remember watching a Louisiana or tricolored heron in the Everglades do what appeared to be a fan dance, utilizing its wings. It was not doing a fan dance, however, but instead casting a shadow on the water. Every fisherman knows that fish are attracted to shadows, and so, apparently, did the bird. Was the behavior of the green heron or the Louisiana heron a learned behavior, handed down from past generations, or was it instinct? Or are there examples of a creature reasoning out a solution to a problem at hand?

James Gould of Princeton University, who has done studies with honeybees, suggests that intelligence in any creature involves "cognitive trial and error"—the thinking through of possible solutions to a problem before actually putting any of them into effect. Gould tried an experiment with honeybees in which he set out a bowl of sugar water for their use. Each day he moved the bowl 25 percent further away from the hive. The bees soon learned to anticipate the exact spot where he would move the bowl. In fact, one day the bees were at the location waiting for the bowl to arrive.

Gould believes this represented a show of intelligence on the part of the bees, since they're not genitically programmed to take advantage of a movable food source. To further his experiment, Gould placed a food source in the middle of a lake. He made sure a scout bee found and reported it to the hive, but the worker bees would not stop at that position. They would fly across the lake, but they would not halt in its midst, indicating that even though food was there, they chose not to take the risk of alighting on a small object floating in the water.

"I feel," said Gould, "that bees have some sort of cognitive map and evaluate information to see if it makes sense before they act on it."

The experience I related earlier—of watching porpoises just off the causeway to Sanibel Island in Florida forming a circle in the water and playing toss with a dead fish—indicates to me that these creatures do indeed think, that they invent games, and that they possess a special camaraderie with other creatures of their own kind.

Dr. Lilly in his experiments with dolphins has found much the same thing. He has told stories of experimenters who tried to train dolphins, but discovered instead that the dolphins

232

Some animal lovers think of animals as just another form of human-type creatures. These muskox were caught on film in Alaska.

233

were training them. An example of this occurred one day when a dolphin was being rewarded with fish for performing tricks. The dolphin obviously enjoyed the game, but soon became sated with fish. It then carried the fish each time to the bottom of the pool, where it stacked them neatly in one corner of the tank.

"When he tired of the experiment," Dr. Lilly recalled, "he just went to the bottom, got a fish, and handed it to the experimenter. Dolphins are fully aware, fully sentient, fully conscious. They possess greater intelligence in my estimation than do humans."

Researchers doing experiments with monkeys have found some interesting indications of intelligence, too. One researcher hung a banana from a ceiling to see if a chimp, already used to boxes, would think of stacking some that were nearby to reach it. The chimp outdid the researcher, however, by grasping his hand and leading him to stand directly under the banana. Then the chimp climbed up on the researcher's shoulders to reach the banana.

Scientists have found that a rhesus monkey adept at problem solving can watch another monkey perform a single trial on a problem and then get it correct himself even if the other monkey got it wrong.

Many scientists believe intelligence is somehow connected with what we call "consciousness"—another quality no one can quite define. Although consciousness does exist, it is not something that can be measured or even located. Consciousness implies, among other things, feelings and willpower—the very characteristics we have in mind when we talk about ourselves.

Says Dr. Lilly: "If we attribute consciousness to other animals, we may well have to treat them as we treat ourselves. And for most people, that's an impossibility."

Lilly points out the importance of consciousness in dolphins. They spend about 99 percent or more of their time under water, he explained, so they are really water beings. This affects their consciousness. When you depend upon the air above you for sustenance, for consciousness, for continuing to

234

live, you make sure your friends are with you, either above you or below you or at the same level as you are. For if anything happens to you—if you should lose consciousness—you must depend upon your friends to bring you to the surface so you can breathe.

A few years ago while working with manatees at Blue Springs State Park in Florida, park rangers were called on an emergency run up the nearby St. Johns River where a passer-by had reported a manatee in trouble. When the rangers arrived on the scene, they found an adult female manatee that had been slashed up by a speeding power boat. Six other manatees had gathered around the injured creature and were holding its head above the surface so it could breathe. They were so protective of the injured creature that these normally docile, nonaggressive creatures tried to keep the rangers from reaching it. A calf, apparently belonging to the wounded cow, swam frantically nearby, obviously upset at what had happened to its mother.

"We learned later," said one ranger, "that the manatee was already dead, but its companions didn't know that and were prepared to help it to the last breath." Afterwards he told me the sea cow had been run over three times, apparently by the same power boat, indicating that whoever had run over it the first time turned around and intentionally ran over it twice more, probably just for kicks. The sea cow, or manatee, is now found only in Florida waters and is on the federal endangered species list.

At any rate, this points up one fact quite positively. Each creature that spends most of its life in or under the water and is dependent upon rising to the surface to breathe has a strong interdependence upon others of its type. And that interdependence only works with very positive communication. Dolphins create vocalization by forcing air back and forth between air sacs inside their bodies. Apparently, without this communication and interdependence, the dolphin, which dates back some 15 million years on this planet, would long ago have joined the dinosaurs, passenger pigeons, and terradactyls as an extinct species.

Do birds, such as this common egret in Florida, think and solve problems?

So, do other creatures possess intelligence? If you believe the answer to be a definite *Yes*, as I do, then it's easy to speculate on the role wild creatures may play in the future of our own sociobiological environment.

People who have had varied experiences with creatures offer varied opinions about the future. One of the most positive forecasts is again suggested by Dr. Lilly, who began to study the brain of the bottle-nosed dolphin in 1955. He believes we may, in time, create a whole new way of communicating based upon our experiences with dolphins.

But Lilly believes the new language will not come about until we, as humans, have been able to open our minds totally and to look at things in an alternate state of consciousness. "We have all heard so much about eternity," he says. "I'd like to propose a word I borrowed from science fiction—alternity, the alternate way of looking at things, alternate states of consciousness. Alternity is a way to look at all the possibilities, not just the probabilities. Many people, particularly young people who have not become locked into a rutted state of mind, can understand. But most of the human race unfortunately does not."

Lilly is now working with dolphins and computers, trying to isolate the sounds formed within the dolphins' frequency range, which is approximately ten times that of humans. The problem, he says, is in getting the dolphins to match the sounds of words, sentences, and expressions until we can finally exchange ideas. Lilly first began to think about the possibilities of establishing another language with dolphins back in the early 1960s when he listened to a tape on a friend's recorder at half speed and suddenly heard a dolphin mimicking his laughter and also electronically generating tones within the room. So he began experimenting—trying to teach a dolphin to speak.

"I shouted at Elvore one morning, 'Squirt water.' He repeated, 'Squeert wadde, squeert.' I said, 'No, squirt water.' And we both worked at it all morning, back and forth, until he got it. The sound was so loud it was piercing. And suddenly I realized this was not just a dolphin, but another incredible life form that was certainly no less than human."

To facilitate a good research and learning process with dolphins, we might do well to develop a space city—not in outer space but in the ocean space—where we could interact with and relate to all the various forms of ocean life. We could call it Dolphin City. Lilly, who is also an MD, has even proposed we consider building houses around the edge of the sea with waterways a couple of feet deep connecting the living room to the water. "The dolphins could then come and observe people, day and night, in their routine lives," he said. "We could even visualize having human mothers in these communities give birth to their babies under water, and the dolphins would be the midwives. This would be the safest way to be born, and it definitely would be the nicest way to be born," he added.

His proposal reiterates one concept already explored by the Soviets. The Russians have had Olympic swimmers who were pregnant giving birth under water with dolphins present. The humans felt no panic or fear—the presence of the dolphins seemed to have dispelled all that. The Soviets even made movies of such scenes to show on television.

Not much of this is likely to happen soon, if ever. We, as members of what we consider to be the superior race, would be very reluctant to stoop to any kind of interdependence upon another creature. And yet if we look around us, we must realize the interdependence of all nature, one thing upon the other. Everything in the universe is connected. As the late John Steinbeck wrote in *The Sea of Cortez:* "It is a good thing for a man to look down at the tide-pools, then up to the stars, then back to the tide-pools again." Some people believe the recognition of interdependence among all things may indeed be the only salvation for mankind.

The idea of dolphins assisting at the birth of humans conceivably might be only the beginning of a whole new relationship. Many other animals, including the dolphins, might be employed in a teaching role as well. Lilly believes it would not only work but is paramount. "When you swim with the dolphins," he says, "you realize right away how well they can teach, without any verbal communication taking place whatsoever."

That teaching ability, the influence dolphins can have, was pointed out in the case discussed earlier in this book involving autistic children in the Miami area and on Key Largo, Florida. "We can learn so much from animals," Lilly emphasizes. "The teaching is not done by preaching or through force. It is done in subtle ways, through showing, observation, even gentle reinforcement."

The more I associate with the wild kingdom and the great outdoors, the more I take the time to observe and study the fiber of life that exists around me in my own woodland and in natural areas around the world, the more I became convinced that animals and indeed all wildlife can teach us much about ourselves, as well as our own environment.

Dian Fossey has spent more than fifteen years studying gorillas in Africa's Rwanda. She believes the benefit of intimate contact on a day-to-day basis suggests that nature is gentle and redemptive. And if nature is gentle, she adds, then our human meanness could turn out to be a passing phase in our own evolution.

The animals, birds, insects, reptiles, fish, and even plants have so much to teach us. The tragedy is we are not likely to listen. The real problem with animal talk may not be that our ethics are challenged by what we hear, but that we aren't open-minded enough to hear at all. Bearhead Sweeney, a tribal leader of the Flathead Indians, defiantly tells skeptical whites: "your culture doesn't understand. It takes a pragmatic and dogmatic attitude and says, 'Prove it!'

"My uncle heard the owls talking," he goes on. "They were making strange sounds, but they were talking Indian talk. My aunt didn't believe him, but they were bringing an omen, a warning. A few weeks later, there was a big landslide and people were killed. That's what the owls were telling him."

Years ago, I went to visit the classroom of a junior high school teacher named George McDuffie in Cincinnati. George

Animals from bees to birds to mammals have exhibited cognitive behavior. These endangered brown pelicans are protected on Pelican Island, Florida.

had made an unusual reputation for himself—and rightly so. He used animals to teach. His biology classes were among the most popular in the entire school system. A visit to the class-room was like a visit to the neighborhood zoo, except that the animals were not caged. A huge monitor lizard more than two feet long roamed around the room constantly. A four-foot al-ligator slept under a desk, and one of the students had her feet propped on its back. A six-foot indigo snake slithered along the window sill. And a bothersome porcupine tried to steal a ribbon from a girl's hair.

Learning in George McDuffie's classroom took on a new dimension. It was not a class that students dreaded entering each day; instead, it was something everyone looked forward to, once they had dispelled their initial fear of the animals and reptiles that roamed there. When alligators were discussed in class, everyone knew exactly what an alligator looked like, what their habits were, how they moved, and how they felt, something many people never learn. But more than that, there was a rapport and understanding which was readily ap-parent, not just on the part of the students toward the animals, but also vice versa. Each accepted the other and learned from the expeience.

During all the years that George McDuffie taught, there was hardly ever an instance of harm done by either the stu-dents or the animals.

At the time I visited the class, I considered the entire situation great folly. Of course it was a neat thing to do, and George McDuffie had established a reputation for himself as a teacher who was different. He had little difficulty holding at-tention in class. But when I thought about it years afterward, McDuffie's classroom took on more meaning. It was an exam-ple of great teaching, a laboratory for learning at first hand about biological life forms other than our own, and it was a lesson in rapport and understanding between humans and other life forms on an almost equal level.

Those of us who have spent much of our lives in the pro-fession of communication realize full well the misconceptions that can occur between peoples speaking the same language.

241

Can we learn to tap the intellectual force that bonds all living things?

Only because more is exchanged than merely the oral or written word is communication at all possible. There must be a conscious feeling, an identity established, and an affinity created. Sometimes we refer to much of our communication as chemistry, or vibrations. Many scoff at the mention of such intangibles, but there is no doubt that these factors do highly influence communication and understanding. When—and only when—we have learned to assign such factors to our communication efforts with other life forms, we can expect to achieve measurable results.

The steps beyond what we now know may indeed be overwhelming. Think of the possibilities. Animals to predict all kinds of disasters—earthquakes, tornadoes, hurricanes, landslides or avalanches, floods, fires. Animals to perform research. Animals to teach us the truths of our universe. We

242

have to learn not only to hear the voices about us but to understand what they are saying. As children, we hear adult voices, but because of the complexity of our own lives and the need for early authority in a contentious world, we are scolded by our elders until we no longer hear because we no longer listen. But the voices are still there. If our society is to survive, we must allow our culture to speak for the intangibles—courage, love, caring, honor—and we must have the fortitude to stand up and let our convictions be heard.

Too often we discourage fantasies and hallucinations. Yet it may only be through such free thinking that we become capable of taking a realistic look at our true selves, of examining the spirit and tapping into the basic intellectual force that bonds all living things. Then we will have achieved a great step forward in understanding the life around us.

List of Prime Wildlife Areas

Literally hundreds of national wildlife refuges; national, regional, state, county, and city parks; and state wildlife areas have been established as ideal wildlife habitat. A complete list may be obtained by contacting the appropriate agencies listed below, or by contacting the various state governments. Some of my favorite wildlife areas in America—chosen in part for the high density or visibility of wildlife and their reasonable accessibility—are listed alphabetically by state.

Wheeler
Box 1643
Decatur, Al 35601

Arctic
101 12th Avenue
Box 20
Fairbanks, AK 99701

Denali National Park
% Alaska Group
P.O. Box 2252
Anchorage, AK 99501

Kenai
P.O. Box 2139
Soldotna, AK 99669

Kodiak
P.O. Box 825
Kodiak, AK 99615

Yukon Delta
P.O. Box 346
Bethel, AK 99559

Yukon Flats
101 12th Avenue
Box 20
Fairbanks, AK 99701

Organ Pipe Cactus
National Monument
P.O. Box 38
Ajo, AZ 85321

Saquero National Monument
P.O. Box 17210
Tucson, AZ 85710

Ano Naevo State Reserve
95 Kelly Avenue
Half Moon Bay, CA 94019

Anza-Borrego State Park
P.O. Box 428
Borrego Springs, CA 92004

Channel Islands
P.O. Box 1388
Oxnard, CA 93030

Condor Sanctuary
Los Padres National Forest
42 Aero Camino St.
Goleta, CA 93017

Death Valley National
Monument
Three Rivers, CA 93271

Havasu
Box A
Needles, CA 92363

Joshua Tree National
Monument
P.O. Box 875
Twentynine Palms, CA
92277

Salton Sea
P.O. Box 120
Calipatria, CA 92223

Sacramento Valley Refuges
Route 1, Box 311
Willows, CA 95988

Arapaho
Box 457
Walden, CO 80480

Bombay Hook
Route 1, Box 147
Smyrna, DE 19977

Everglades National Park
P.O. Box 279
Homestead, FL 33030

J.N. "Ding" Darling
P.O. Drawer B
Sanibel, FL 33957

Loxahatchee
Box 278, RI
Boynton, Beach, FL 33437

Merritt Island
Box 6504
Titusville, FL 32780

National Key Deer
Box 510
Big Pine Key, FL 33043

St. Vincent
Box 447
Apalachicola, FL 32320

Okefenokee
Box 117
Waycross, GA 31501

Hawaiian & Pacific
Islands Refuge
P.O. Box 50167
300 Ala Moana Blvd.
Honolulu, HI 96850

Crab Orchard
Box J
Cartersville, IL 62918

Jasper-Pulaski State
Wildlife Refuge
Medaryville, IN 47957

Muscatatuck
Box 631
Seymour, IN 47274

Flint Hills
Box 128
Hartford, KS 66854

Delta-Breton
Venice, LA 70091

Lacassine
Route 1, Box 186
Lake Arthur, LA 70549

Acadia National Park
Rt. 1 Box 1
Bar Harbor, ME 04609

Moosehorn
Box X
Calais, ME 04619

Blackwater
Route 1, Box 121
Cambridge, MD 21613

Eastern Neck
Route 2, Box 225
Rock Hall, MD 21661

Parker River
Northern Blvd. Plum Island
Newburyport, MA 01950

Monomoy
Northern Blvd., Plum Island
Newburyport, MA 01950

Isle Royale National Park
87 N. Ripley Street
Houghton, MI 49931

Upper Mississippi River
Wildlife & Fish Refuge
Hdqts.
51 E. 4th Street
Winona, MN 55987

Mississippi Sandhill
Crane Complex
2509 Westgate Pkwy
Gautier, MS 39553

Mingo
Route 1, Box 103
Puxico, MO 63960

Glacier National Park
West Glacier, MT 59936

National Bison Range
Moiese, MT 59824

Fort Niobrara
Hidden Timber Route
Valentine, NE 69201

Desert National Wildlife
Refuge
1500 N. Decatur Blvd.
Las Vegas, NV 89108

Brigantine
Great Creek Road, Box 72
Oceanville, NJ 08231

Great Swamp
Pleasant Plains Rd.
Rd 1, Box 148
Basking Ridge, NJ 07920

Bosque del Apache
Box 1246
Socorro, NM 87801

Carlsbad Caverns
P.O. Box 1598
Carlsbad, NM 88220

Guadalupe Mountains
℅ Carlsbad Caverns
P.O. Box 1598
Carlsbad, NM 88220

White Sands National
Monument
Box 458
Alamagordo, NM 88310

Pea Island
Box 150
Rodanthe, NC 27968

Audubon
Rural Route 1
Coleharbor, ND 58531

Wichita Mountains Wildlife
Route 1, Box 448
Indiahoma, OK 73552

Hart Mountain National
Antelope Refuge,
Box 111
Room 308, U.S. P.O. Bldg.
Lakeview, OR 97630

Malheur
P.O. Box 113
Burns, OR 97720

Salt Meadow
Box 307
Charlestown, RI 02813

Cape Romain
Route 1, Box 191
Awendaw, SC 29429

Custer State Park
Black Hills
Hermosa, SD 57744

Reelfoot
Box 98
Samburg, TN 38254

Aransas
Box 100
Austwell, TX 77950

Big Bend National Park
Tx 79834

Laguna Atascosa
Box 450
Rio Hondo, TX 78583

Chincoteague
Box 62
Chincoteague, VA 23336

Great Dismal Swamp
680B Carolina Rd.
Suffolk, VA 23434

Mason Neck
9502 Richmond Highway
Suite A
Lorton, VA 22079

Olympic National Park
600 E. Park Avenue
Port Angeles, WA 98362

Horicon
Route 2
Mayville, WI 53050

Grand Teton National Park
P.O. Box 67
Moose, WY 83012

National Elk Refuge
Box C
Jackson WY 83001

Yellowstone National Park
WY 82190

Photo Workshops

The author conducts several annual nature and wildlife photojournalism training seminars in some of the world's remaining "wild places," including Africa, Alaska, and Antarctica. And programs take place in the forty-eight contiguous states:

Everglades, Big Cypress and 10,000 Islands, Florida, March.

Okefenokee, St. Marys River and Cumberland Island, Georgia, April.

Seminar of the Sea off Maine and Bay of Fundy, September.

Seminar of the Desert in Arizona, November.

Workshops include instruction in nature and wildlife photography, building rapport with other life forms, tracking, stalking, using blinds, capturing spirit. For further information, write to Box 51532, Indianapolis, IN 46251.

INDEX

Adams, Ansel, 185
Adders, 20
Aerial photography, 198, 199–201
Aesop, 227
Agfachrome film, 191
Alaska Fish & Game Commission, 157
Alligators, 58, 227
Alternity, 237
American Indians
    hunting and, 65–69
    reverence toward animals of, 50, 57, 63–68
    tracking and, 118
    walking and, 104, 105
Animal Thinking (Griffin), 231
Anpsi, 160
Antelope, 32, 68
Ants, 33, 46
Aristotle, 170
Arizona-Sonora Desert Museum, 214, 216, 229
Art, animals in, 26–27, 49, 50, 63
Audubon Magazine, 73, 75

Audubon Society, 87, 89
Australian black snakes, 20
Autistic children, dolphins and, 158, 209–210, 211–213, 239

Backster, Cleve, 172–174
Backster Research Foundation, 174
Bank, John, 162
Bateson, G., 213–214
Bats, 141
Bears, 12, 15, 68, 160, 212, 215
    grizzly, 92, 154–157, 160, 161, 210–211
    Kodiak, 155, 157–158
    scent of, 142, 145–147
Bears and I, The (Leslie), 59
Beavers, 95, 121
Bees, 15, 38–40, 46, 232
Beesley, Lloyd, 51
Beetles, 15
Behavior (journal), 204
Bender, Dr. Hans, 163
Bengal tigers, 53
Bible, the, 27, 49, 226

Big game hunters, 73
Bighorn desert sheep, 70, 146
Birds, 12, 19, 23, 33, 43, 129
  handicapped persons and, 24
  territorial instincts of, 31–32
  see also names of birds
Bison, 26, 65, 68, 103
"Bitter Harvest" (Mitchell), 73
Black bears, 160
Blinds (concealments), 98–100
  for photography, 194–195
Bluejays, 86, 151–154
Blue Springs State Park, 235
Bobcats, 83, 110, 139
  tracking, 126–128, 129, 130
Boone, J. Allen, 57, 58
Boredom of zoo animals, 216–220
Bowerbirds, 19
Box turtles, 122
Bronx Zoo, 217
Brookfield Zoo, 217
Brooks, Carolyn, 209–210
Brown, Tom, Jr., 40, 55, 79, 112,
    116, 119, 122, 131
Brown pelicans, 111, 144, 221, 240
Bullfrogs, 28
Bull moose, 37, 47, 117
Burbank, Luther, 168, 180–182
Butterflies, 23
  monarch, 15, 16, 112–113

California condors, 26, 220
Cameras, 187–188, 196
  practicing with, 192
  underwater, 199
Camouflage clothing, 93, 179,
    195–196
Canada geese, 24, 43–46, 166, 201
Cape buffalo, 73
Caribou, 102
Carnarvon, Lord, 163
Caron, Joan, 206, 209
Carver, George Washington, 168
Carvings, cave, 50
Caterpillars, 148

Cats
  hearing sense of, 138
  instinct and, 160
  as sacred animals, 27
Cave art, 26, 49, 50, 63
Chemical communication, see
    Pheromones
Chimpanzees, 19, 37, 38
Chipmunks, 31, 140
Coatimundi, 159
Cody, Buffalo Bill, 68
Connell, Richard, 76
Consciousness, 59
  intelligence and, 234–237
Copperheads, 20
Corson, Dr. Samuel, 24
Cottonmouth moccasins, 16
Cougars, 42, 110
Coyotes, 19, 31
Cranes, 100
Crocodiles, 27
Cronkite, Walter, 178
Crows, 25, 31, 86
Cummings, Dr. William, 43

Darwin, Charles, 170
Deer, 23, 31, 68, 96
  demarcating domain of, 32
  hearing sense of, 134, 135, 138
  instinct and, 154
  intelligence of, 17
  Key, 218
  mule, 110
  stalking, 112
  touching among, 37
  tracking, 121–122, 131
  whitetail, 31, 34, 62, 71, 75, 76,
    85, 112, 129, 140, 154
Demarcating domain, 32
Desbiez, Marie, 180
Desmond, Tim, 207–209
Dialects among animals, 43
Disney, Walt, 227
Dogs, 19
  instinct and, 161–162, 163, 165

therapeutic value of, 24
Dolphins, 205–206, 233–234
  autistic and retarded children
    and, 158, 209–210,
    211–213, 239
  intelligence of, 234–235, 237
  language of, 237–238
  touching among, 37–38
Droppings (scat), 83, 118, 131
Ducks Unlimited, 75

Eagles, 26, 65, 67, 102
Earthquakes, animal sensitivity and,
    163–166
Egypt (ancient), 27, 63, 226
Eiseley, Loren, 62
Ektachrome film, 191
Elephants, 73, 79
Elephant seals, 13
Elk, 12, 68, 73, 79, 96
Endangered species, 50–51, 71,
    220, 221, 240
Esser, Dr. Aristide, 163
Ethology, 14, 27, 42, 46
Everglades, 12, 58, 201
Exercises for walking and stalking,
    115–116
Extrasensory perception (ESP), 151,
    158–159
  plants and, 170–171
Eye contact, 36, 211

Falcons, peregrine, 30
Fer-de-lances, 20
Field & Stream Magazine, 78, 126
*Field Guide to Tracking and Nature
    Observation, A* (Brown), 55
Film for cameras, 191–192
Finches, 30
Fish, 134–137, 160–161
Food plants, 193
Fossey, Dian, 239
Fournier, George, 222
Foxes
  gray, 91–93, 129

red, 82, 106, 129
France, Raoul, 170
Freud, Sigmund, 46–48
Frisch, Karl von, 38–40
Frogs, 28, 30, 122
  dialects of, 43

Gaddy, Hazel, 44
Gaddy, Lockhart, 43–44
Gaddy's Wild Goose Refuge, 44,
    164, 167
Geese, Canada, 24, 43–46, 166,
    201
Golden orb spiders, 200
Goodall, Jane, 19, 38
Gorillas, 239
Gould, James, 232
Gray fox, 91–93, 129
Gray whales, 61, 201
Great Swamp National Wildlife Re-
    fuge, 24, 154
Greece (ancient), 63, 226
Green mambas, 20
Griffin, Donald R., 231
Grizzly bears, 92, 154–157, 160,
    161, 210–211
Groupers, 136–137
Grouse, 31, 128, 129
Guravich, Dan, 112–113

Haast, William, 214, 229
Halas, John, 136
Hammerhead sharks, 201
Handbook of PSI Discoveries (Os-
    trander and Schroeder), 173
Handicapped persons
  bird watching and, 24
  therapeutic value of pets for,
    23–24
  see also Autistic children; Re-
    tarded children
Hanson, Guy, 165
Hasler, Dr. A. D., 161
Hawks, 19, 31, 102

Hearing sense, 134, 135, 138, 141–143
Herons, 231–232
  Louisiana, 45, 149
  white, 153
Hibernation, 15–16
Hippopotamus, 48
Homing ability, 160–162
Honey badger (ratel), 33
Honeybees, 38–40, 46, 232
Honey dance, 38–40
Honey guide (bird), 33
Hoosier National Forest, 87, 128
Howard, Eliot, 31
Hummingbirds, 16
Humpback whales, dialects of, 43
Hunting, 62–80
  American Indians and, 65–69
  positive and negative aspects of, 75–76
  three basic types, 72–75
Hyenas, 19

Ibis, 27
Indian licorice plant, 171
Indians, see American Indians
Insects, 38, 46
  hearing sense of, 141–143
Instinct, 12, 20, 151–166
  anpsi, 160
  bears and, 154–158, 160
  deer and, 154
  earthquakes and, 165–166
  fish and, 160–161
Institute of Ecology, 56
Intelligence
  in animals, 229–237
  difficulty of measuring, 229–230
In the Shadow of Man (Goodall), 38
Island, The (Thomas), 154

John Pennekamp State Park, 136

Keeton, William, 165
Kellert, Stephen, 72

Key deer, 218
Killer whales, 206–207, 208, 209
King cobras, 20
Kinship with All Life (Boone), 59
Kipling, Rudyard, 49
Knee bends, 116
Kodachrome film, 191
Kodiak bears, 155, 157–158
Kodiak Island, 154
Kozicky, Edward, 72

Language, see Talk
Larkin, Timy, 165
Lascaux Cave, 26, 49
Lawler, Dr. Howard, 216, 229
Lenses, camera, 188–189
Leopards, 73
Leslie, Robert Franklin, 59–60, 178
Light, as primary element of photography, 196–198
Lilly, Dr. John, 205–206, 210, 233–234, 237–239
Linné, Carl von, 170
Lions, 73, 110
Listening (hearing), 133–145
Lobo wolves, 41
Lorenz, Konrad, 27, 46
Louisiana herons, 45, 149

Macaque monkeys, 42–43
McDuffie, George, 239–241
Madson, John, 72
Magnetic electrodes, 14
Manatees (sea cows), 15, 33, 36, 207
  intelligence of, 235
Marineland, 207, 209
Marmots, 18
Mating habits, 83
Mayans, 63
Meat hunters, 72, 75
Mesopotamia, 27
Miami Seaquarium, 205, 206, 208
Miami Serpentarium, 214
Migration, 15–16

Mind in the Waters (Bateson), 213–214
Minks, 121
Mirror lens, 189
Mitchell, John, 73, 75
Moccasins (footwear), 107
Moisture, photography and, 197–198
Monarch butterfly, 15, 16
stalking, 112–113
Monkeys
intelligence of, 234
language of, 42–43
Moorten, Patricia, 180
Moorten's Desertland Botanical Garden, 180
Moose, 12, 37, 47, 68, 88, 96–98, 117
Moral code of man, natural laws and, 227–229
Morris, John, 33
Mosquitoes, 141
Most Dangerous Game, The (Connell), 76–78
Motion, as primary element of photography, 196, 198
Mountain lions, 110
Mufflers for cameras, 189
Muir, John, 69, 104
Mule deer, 110
Murie, Olaus J., 119
Music for plants, 174–178
Muskoxen, 114, 233
Muskrats, 121
My Life in the Wild (Tors), 59

National Shooting Sports Foundation, 73
National Zoo, 216
Natural disturbances, animal sensitivity and, 163–166
Natural laws, man's moral code and, 227–229
Nature hunters, 73, 75
New England Aquarium, 33–35

Nolan, Dr. Raymond, 222

Observation (seeing), 12, 13, 81–103
basic methods of, 89–93
blinds for, 98–100, 194–195
body movements and, 93–96
camouflage clothing for, 93
importance of patience, 100–102
pheromones and, 94
Odors, see Scents
Odum, Dr. Eugene, 56, 57
Okefenokee Swamp, 227
Opossums, 83, 121, 129
Osis, Dr. Karlis, 162
Ostrander, Sheila, 173, 174
Otters, 12, 19, 121
Ovenbirds, 30
Owls, 31

Panchatantra, The, 226
Pane, Rapp, 62
Pelicans, 99
brown, 111, 144, 221, 240
Peregrine falcons, 30
Petersen, Dr. Michael, 42–43
Peterson Field Guide to Animal Tracks (Murie), 119
Pets, therapeutic value of, 23–24
Pheasants, 21
Phelan, Jim, 137
Pheromones, 12, 14–15, 18, 46–48, 94
Philodendron, 173–174, 180
Phoenix Zoo, 219
Photography, 184–202
blinds for, 194–195
camouflage clothing for, 195–196
light and motion and, 196–198
stalking techniques and, 194
Photo workshops and seminars, 188, 248
Pigeons, 19, 220–222
Plants, 168–182, 186
ESP and, 170–171

Plants *(cont.)*
  external stimuli and, 14
  food plants, 193
  instant responses of, 171–174
  music for, 174–178
  for nesting, 197
  protective sense of, 178–180
  scent of, 147–148
"Plight of the Swampers, The"
      (Thomas), 78
Poachers, 75
Poglayen, Dr. Inga, 214–216
Porpoises, 204
  work skills of, 222
Positive reinforcement (operant con-
      ditioning), 206–209, 217
Prairie dogs, 56, 97, 181
Pre-Columbian era, animal worship
      in, 26
Prehistoric drawings of animals and
      birds, 26
Pryor, Karen, 216, 217
Psychic Power of Animals, The
      (Schul), 162–163
Ptarmigans, 90, 230
Pushups, 116
Pygmy rattlesnakes, 12

Queen Anne's lace, 148

Rabbits, 31, 51, 129, 140
  stalking, 112
  tracking, 122
Raccoons, 10, 83, 121, 122, 129
Rats, 222
Rattlesnakes, 9–12, 20, 22–23
Red fox, 82, 106, 129
Red-tailed hawks, 31
Reed, Theodore, 216, 217
Religion, animal worship in, 26–27,
      63–68
Research Center for Animal Com-
      munications, 12, 158
Retallack, Dorothy, 176–178
Retarded children, dolphins and,
      158, 209–210, 211–213, 239

Rhine, Dr. J. B., 162
Rhinoceros, 73
Rhoades, David, 178, 180
Rome (ancient), 63, 226
Rooster pheasants, 21
Roth, Lou, 206–207, 208

Salmon, 15–16, 46, 160–161
Salt blocks, 98
Sandhill cranes, 100
San Diego Wild Animal Park, 216
Sasquatch (Bigfoot), 63, 124
Scents, 12, 145–150
  pheromones as means of com-
      munication, 14–15, 46–48
  territorial demarcation and, 32
  vegetarians and, 15
Schroeder, Lynn, 173–174
Schul, Bill, 162–163
Schultz, Jack, 178, 180
Science fiction, 226
Scratchings as signs, 131
Sea lions, 222
Seals, 13, 39
  talking, 33–35, 39, 203–204
Sea of Cortez, The (Steinbeck), 238
Sebeok, Dr. Thomas, 12–13, 158
Seeing, *see* Observation
Seton, Ernest Thompson, 91
Seton method of observation, 91–93
Sharks, 15, 201
Sheepdogs, 65
Shoes for proper walking, 105–107
Shrews, 129
Shutterbug Ads (periodical), 188
Sierra Club, 104
Signs, reading, *see* Tracking
Silent communication, 40–42
Situps, 116
Sixth sense, *see* Instinct
Skinner, Dr. B. F., 27–29, 206, 220
Skunk cabbage, 148
Skunks, 121, 129, 145
Smith, Dr. Betsy, 209, 210,
      211–213
Smith, George, 175

Snakes, 9–12, 20, 22–23, 134
  cottonmouth moccasin, 16
  intelligence of, 20–23, 214, 229
  rattlesnakes, 9–12, 20, 22–23
  spreadhead viper, 140
  tracking, 122
Songbirds, 129
Sparrows, 30
Sperm whales, 206
Spiders, 200
Sport hunters, 72–73
Spreadhead viper (hognose), 140
Squirrels, 23, 30, 129, 140
  stalking, 112
Stalking, 109–116
  exercises for, 115–116
  photographing and, 194
  stalking movements, 110–115
Statues of animals, 27
Steel, Cathy, 33
Steinbeck, John, 238
Stimson, Joni, 219
Super-sensitive perception (SSP),
    171, 172–173
Swallow, Alice, 203–204
Swallow, George, 203–204
Swamp, The (Thomas), 12, 112
Swans, 223
Sweeney, Bearhead, 239

Talk (language), 30–48
  crows and, 31
  deer and, 31
  dolphins and, 237–238
  manatees and, 33
  seals and, 33–35, 39, 203–204
  silence as, 40–42
  wolves and, 35–36
Teachers, animals as, 242–243
Teale, Edwin Way, 100
Telephoto lens, 188–189
35mm single-lens reflex (SLR) cam-
    eras, 187, 188, 196
Thomas, Bill, Jr., 181
Thomas, David, 76, 77, 78
Thoreau, Henry David, 69, 91

Tigers, 110
  Bengal, 53
Tinbergen, Niko, 27
Tom Brown's Wilderness Survival
    & Tracking School, 32, 108,
    115, 190
Tors, Ivan, 59
Totemic animals, 26–27, 65
Totem poles, 65
Touching
  among animals, 37–38
  by humans, 38, 148–150
Tracking, 83, 118–132
  identification of tracks, 119–122
  in winter, 74
Tracking sticks, 121–122
Training animals, 203–224
  building confidence and, 209–214
  eliminating boredom and,
    216–220
  positive reinforcement and,
    206–209, 217
  work skills and, 220–224
Trees, 178–180
Tree stands, 195
Trophy hunters, 73

Underwater photography, 19,
    198–199
Unexpected Universe, The
    (Eiseley), 62
U.S. Fish & Wildlife Service, 50,
    69, 195

Vegetarians, 15
Vegetation, disturbance of, 132
Verhave, Dr. Thom, 220–222
Vogel, Marcel, 180
Vultures, 19

Waggle dance, 40
Walking, 104–109, 115–116
  exercises for, 115–116
  foot contact, 105–109
  shoes for, 105–107
Waterfowl habitats, 75